The Land
That Slept Late

S0-AFE-319

The Land That Slept Late

The Olympic Mountains in Legend and History

by Robert L. Wood

THE
MOUNTAINEERS

Published by
The Mountaineers
1001 SW Klickitat Way, Suite 201
Seattle, Washington 98134

© 1995 by Robert L. Wood

All rights reserved

8 7 6 5
5 4 3 2 1

No part of this book may be reproduced in any form, or by any
electronic, mechanical, or other means, without permission in
writing from the publisher.

Published simultaneously in Canada by Douglas & McIntyre, Ltd.,
1615 Venables Street, Vancouver, B.C. V5L 2H1
Published simultaneously in Great Britain by Cordee, 3a DeMontfort
Street, Leicester, England, LE1 7HD

Manufactured in Canada

Edited by Pat Coburn
Maps by Jerry Painter
Cover and book design by The Mountaineers Books
Typography by The Mountaineers Books
Book layout by Michelle Taverniti

Cover photographs: *Mountaineers descending the Middle Peak of Mount Olympus, 1913 outing* (Photo by Mabel Furry, courtesy Special Collections, University of Washington Libraries, neg. no. 15273)
Inset (front and back): *The Olympic Mountains* (Photo by Robert L. Wood)

Frontispiece: *Goblin Gates* (Photo by Frank O. Shaw)

Library of Congress Cataloging-in-Publication Data
Wood, Robert L.
    The land that slept late : the Olympic Mountains in legend and
history / by Robert L. Wood.
        p.   cm.
    Includes bibliographical references (p.   ) and index.
    ISBN 0-89886-440-2
    1. Olympic Mountains (Wash.)—History. 2. Legends—
Washington (State)—Olympic Mountains. 3. Olympic National
Park (Wash.)—History. I. Title.
F897.05W625   1995
979.7'94—dc20   95–33199
                                                          CIP

♻ Printed on recycled paper

For Tom and Jessica

CONTENTS

Acknowledgments

In writing this book, I have drawn upon almost a half-century of intimate acquaintance with the Olympic Mountains, and to acknowledge everyone who has provided assistance would be virtually impossible. Because I have relied heavily upon my own books—particularly those on the Press and O'Neil expeditions—anyone whose aid or help has been noted in those publications can consider that he or she is acknowledged here.

The late Preston P. Macy and Will Muller wrote an article about the Press Expedition entitled "The Land that Slept Late," which was published in the December 1946 issue of American Forests, and I now take this opportunity to credit them for having provided not only the title, but also the inspiration, for this book.

I especially wish to thank the anonymous, dedicated librarians of the Seattle Public Library and the University of Washington Libraries, who were most helpful. My sincere thanks go to Karyl Winn, the University Archivist, and her staff; to Richard H. Engeman, Photographs and Graphics Librarian, and Sandra Kroupa, Book Arts Librarian, Special Collections and Preservation Division, University of Washington Allen Library; to Janet E. Baldwin, Curator of Collections, the Explorers Club; to Susan Schultz, historian, National Park Service, Port Angeles, Washington; to Ella Fitzgerald, Alaska Historical Collections, Alaska State Library; and to Kim Molitor, Stearns County Historical Society, St. Cloud, Minnesota.

I am grateful to Grace Lapham of Olympia and Lelia Barney of Tenino for the photograph of John J. Banta, their stepgrandfather.

I am indebted to Tim McNulty for calling my attention to the 1878 Watkinson Expedition, and to David L. Nicandri, Director, Washington State Historical Society, for suggestions regarding condensation of portions of the text.

And finally, I wish to thank Thomas N. Tonne, my "surrogate grandson," and his wife, Jessica, for their encouragement and interest in this project. I feel especially indebted to Jessica, who very capably word-processed the manuscript (which I had typed on an old-fashioned typewriter) onto a computer disk.

—Robert L. Wood
October 1994

1

The Land That Slept Late

THE OLYMPIC PENINSULA, A QUADRANgular chunk of land comprising the northwestern corner of Washington State (and, concurrently, the northwestern corner of the "Lower 48" states) lies about midway between the Equator and the North Pole on the western coast of North America. Approximately sixty-five hundred square miles in extent, it is bounded on the west, north, and east by, respectively, the Pacific Ocean, the Strait of Juan de Fuca, and Puget Sound. Only on the south, where the peninsula is linked to the mainland between Grays Harbor and Puget Sound, does its boundary become indefinite.

About half of the peninsula—its central core—is occupied by the Olympic Mountains, a cluster of peaks, ridges and spurs about sixty miles in diameter. This chaotic mass is slashed by deep canyons cut by rivers that spiral outward from the center. The snow-clad peaks rise abruptly from near sea level to heights of almost eight thousand feet. Not high as mountains go, they are nonetheless impressive, their lower flanks clothed with virgin forests, their summits capped with snowfields and glaciers. Geologically, the mountains are still youthful, their origins going back only 120 million years.

Because they stand between the Pacific Ocean and Puget Sound, the Olympics are highly visible on clear days. Nevertheless, they constitute a land that slept late insofar as human activities go. In fact, the mountains long remained *terra incognita,* one of the least known regions in the United States.

According to archaeologists, Indians whose ancestors came from Asia resided on the Olympic Peninsula at least twelve thousand years before the first Europeans arrived. No one knew, when the Caucasians appeared, exactly how long the "Native Americans" had occupied the land because they had no written language, calendars, or "recorded history." They did have, however, an "oral history" that was based upon traditions—handed down by word

of mouth from one generation to the next—which indicates that the Indians may have lived there longer and explored the land more extensively than the Caucasians supposed. (The problem with oral history is that the events related almost invariably become modified or distorted with the passage of time, thus making it difficult, if not impossible, to distinguish fact from fiction or myth.) Complicating the picture is the fact that the Indians trod lightly upon the land, not roughshod like the white man, and thus they left little evidence of their passage. They did not "build" trails (like the white man does); they simply created paths with their feet (like the elk do), and such paths blended so well into the landscape that, to inexperienced eyes, they were not readily discernible.

Nevertheless, the Caucasians who came to the peninsula in the middle and late nineteenth century invariably reported the Indians feared and shunned the remote interior, and seldom went into that district. For example, Eldridge Morse, writing about 1880 for historian Hubert Howe Bancroft with respect to Washington's territorial days, stated: "The Indians are not known to have ever crossed the wild Olympic Mountains, either from north to south, or from east to west, they always went around." If logic is the determining factor, Morse's statement is undoubtedly correct. The Olympics are a rounded cluster of rugged peaks and ridges, not a "barrier range" as such; consequently, one can

Terra incognita: *the central Olympics* (Photo courtesy Pacific Aerial Surveys, Inc.)

go around them with much less effort than traveling directly across them from one side to the other.

One legend suggests another reason why the Indians may not (at least in recent centuries) have ventured far into the Olympics. This myth holds that a river flowed through beautiful vales where, in ancient times, the various tribes held meetings and pursued peaceful endeavors, such as trading and athletic games. However, Seatco, a god, became angry and shook the earth, thus destroying the valley and most of its inhabitants. The earthquake's survivors, fearing Seatco's wrath and vengeance, shunned the interior from that time.

According to the Indians' religious traditions, the high peaks were the abode of the Thunderbird, whose lofty eyrie lay hidden among the crags of Mount Olympus. The Makah Indians, for example, believed this deity appeared in the form of a gigantic Indian whose raiment consisted of a bird's head, a pair of large wings, and feathers to cover his body. He resembled a raven or eagle and was large enough to darken the heavens. His body was the thunder cloud, the flapping of his wings created thunder, and lightning was either the flashing of his eyes or bolts of fire expelled from his tongue. A respected being of strength and force in many

Makah Indian women wearing tribal regalia (Photo courtesy National Park Service)

traditions, the Thunderbird was often sought for its power by those who had undergone the appropriate preparation.

The Native Americans were oriented more to the sea than they were to the land, and invariably they lived near salt water. They traveled chiefly by canoe, and usually did not go far on foot. Their hunting trips were generally confined to the lowlands, but tribal legends do tell of journeys to higher-elevation hot springs, and of expeditions to the "land of snow and ice" in pursuit of elk, deer, and bear. Actually, the Indians had little reason to visit the mountains. The climate along the shores was mild, fish and shellfish were abundant, and the people obtained berries as well as game from the forests near their homes.

The fact that the Indians feared and avoided the interior of the peninsula undoubtedly helped to establish the "veil of mystery" that shrouded the Olympics during "the pioneer years." Although the peninsula is no longer mysterious and unknown, it remains sparsely populated, despite its nearness to business and population centers and the fact that, except for its rugged central wilderness, it has been heavily exploited.

Virtually untouched for decades, the peninsula was one of the first regions in the Pacific Northwest with which Europeans came in contact. This was partly because of its position between Puget Sound and the Pacific Ocean, adjacent to the paths of commerce. The acquaintance was casual, however, and the land almost inaccessible except from the sea. The dense forests and lack of navigable streams closed the area to all but a few hunters, trappers, and prospectors. Not until trails and roads were built, early in the twentieth century, did the interior become readily accessible.

The records of a Spanish sailor named Juan Perez contain the oldest known references to the Olympic Mountains. On August 10 and 11, 1774, while sailing south along the coast in search of a strait said to have been discovered in 1592 by a Greek pilot who used the Spanish name Juan de Fuca, Perez and his crew viewed a snowy peak and christened it *La Sierra de la Santa Rosalia.* This was apparently the first time Europeans had viewed the peak; it was also the first place name given by Europeans to a geographic feature in what is now Washington State. During this voyage, Perez "gained the honor of having discovered practically the whole Northwest Coast," and he "had given to his nation whatever of credit and territorial claims may be founded on the mere act of first discovery."

The next year, Spain sought more information about the land Perez had seen by sending out an expedition under Bruno Heceta and Juan Francisco de la Bodega y Quadra. This expedition scrutinized the coast as far north as Alaska. On July 14, 1775, Heceta anchored his schooner, the *Santiago,* off the western coast of the peninsula and went ashore with three of his officers "and a few sailors." Apparently, they were the first Europeans to set foot "on the soil of the Northwest Coast." The men erected a cross and buried a sealed bottle which not only contained a record of the landing, but also formally claimed the region for Spain. Meanwhile, not far to the north, Quadra's sister ship, the schooner *Sonora,* lay at anchor to the lee of an offshore island. Indians approached the ship and held up bits of metal to indicate they wished to barter. Believing they were friendly, Quadra sent the boatswain and six men ashore to obtain fresh water and fuel, but the Indians killed them and destroyed their boat. Quadra signalled Heceta, asking permission to land with a large party and punish the natives, but this was denied. The Spaniards then sailed away, and Quadra named the island *Isla de Dolores,* or Island of Sorrows.

The English arrived shortly after the Spanish left. Captain James Cook explored the northwest coast of North America to establish English sovereignty. While hunting for the Northwest Passage in 1778, during his third voyage, Cook sighted a headland and island between latitudes 48° and 49° north. Although he noted what appeared to be a small opening here—which flattered the sailors with hopes of finding a harbor—Cook did not approach closely because the shore looked dangerous. He named the headland Cape Flattery, and noted that geographers had placed "the pretended Strait of Juan de Fuca" at that latitude, but also stated that he saw no such waterway and didn't think it existed. Inexplicably, Cook failed to recognize the entrance when he saw it. He then sailed northward to Vancouver Island.

Captain Charles Barkley, commanding an East India Company ship, sailed southward from Vancouver Island in 1787 and discovered both Barkley Sound and the Strait of Juan de Fuca. Although he recognized the latter as the Greek sailor's long-lost channel, he did not enter it, but continued on past Cape Flattery. When opposite the mouth of a large river, he anchored near the place where Quadra had met disaster twelve years earlier. Like Quadra, he sent men ashore in a small boat to obtain fresh water, and they, too, were murdered by the Indians. Barkley therefore called the stream Destruction River. However, this name was later given to the nearby island, and the river named for the Hoh Indians who lived in the vicinity.

During the late eighteenth century, European traders arrived in ever-increasing numbers in the Pacific Northwest to obtain furs, at the same time claiming the region for their respective homelands. Among them was Captain John Meares, a British mariner who abandoned his search for the Northwest Passage to engage in the fur trade. He explored the Strait of Juan de Fuca,

A Makah Indian at Neah Bay (Photo courtesy National Park Service)

Gilbert Sotomish, Quinault Indian guide (Photo by the author)

and while so engaged was welcomed by an Indian chief who was fishing with his people at an island near Cape Flattery. Meares named it Tatoosh Island to honor the chief. On July 4, 1788, he sighted the high, snowy peak that Perez had called *Santa Rosalia*. He may have been unaware that the Spaniard had named it, or perhaps he just ignored the fact. At any rate, he considered the peak a worthy dwelling place for the New World's gods, and therefore called it Mount Olympus, after the abode of the Greek deities. The name stuck and the mountain is still so known today.

About this time Spain made a final attempt to retain its waning influence by dispatching Lieutenants Francisco de Eliza, Salvador Fidalgo, and Manuel Quimper to the Pacific Northwest, with instructions to explore the country, build forts, establish harmonious relations with the natives, and not disturb the traders.

As a consequence, Quimper explored the San Juan Islands as well as the coast in the vicinity of present-day Port Townsend, and De Eliza entered the harbor of what is now Port Angeles and also established a base at Discovery Bay. Fidalgo arrived at Neah Bay in 1792, built a fort, and began a settlement: the first one established by Europeans in what is now Washington State. With this act, the Spanish solidified their claim to the Olympic Peninsula. The location was poor, however, and following a dispute with the Indians, the Spanish abandoned the post. Other than on Nootka Sound, on the western coast of Vancouver Island, this was their only attempt to settle in the Pacific Northwest.

Meanwhile, the British strengthened their claims to the country by sending Captain George Vancouver to survey the Northwest coast. He had been a midshipman with Captain Cook in 1778, when Cook failed to recognize the Strait of Juan de Fuca. He now had several assignments. He was to determine if the legendary "River of the West" flowed into the North Pacific; if so, he was to explore the stream and claim the land for England. He would then sail north to Nootka Sound, mapping the coast en route, and declare that territory an English possession as well. Upon arriving at Nootka, he would confer with Quadra, the Spanish representative, and they were to decide which nation owned the continent that bordered the North Pacific. At this time the Spanish claimed the entire Northwest coast. When Vancouver and Quadra conferred, neither side would yield to the other, but both agreed not to claim any rights of sovereignty to the exclusion of the other. The practical effect of this agreement was that they had finally settled the issue by abandoning Nootka to the Indians!

Vancouver sailed into the Strait of Juan de Fuca in 1792. His party explored Puget Sound and took possession of the region for England, calling it New Georgia. Vancouver named many natural features: bodies of water, capes, headlands, inlets, and mountain peaks. He also followed the precedent set by Meares in the naming of Mount Olympus: he, too, ignored Spanish nomenclature, and slapped down the name "Olympic Mountains" on his charts. The Indian names were alike disregarded. Eventually, the "Olympic" designation was extended to the peninsula itself.

The chief representative of the United States in the North Pacific at this time was Captain Robert Gray, who engaged in the sea otter trade for New England merchants. His ship was the *Columbia*. Gray arrived in Nootka Sound in the autumn of 1788, and, like Meares, he wintered there. The following year he sailed fifty miles into the Strait of Juan de Fuca. During the momentous year 1792—the tricentennial of Columbus's discovery of the Americas—Gray sailed southward from Nootka Sound. He sighted the mouth of a large river, but the strong current prevented his entering the stream. During the return trip, Gray met Vancouver and told him he suspected a big river flowed into the Pacific Ocean at Cape Disappointment. He returned later to make another attempt at entry. During this voyage he discovered Grays Harbor, where he landed and proclaimed the sovereignty of the United States. Four days later he sailed into the mouth of the Columbia, the "Great River of the West," which he named for his ship.

Gray's discoveries were significant in that they helped establish American claims to the territory north of the Columbia River. His findings, together with those of Vancouver, set the stage for a struggle, lasting several decades, between England and America for possession of the Oregon country (the Spanish influence had declined about the time the Americans arrived). Gray's discovery of the Columbia also closed the book on discoveries by sea. Subsequently, explorers and adventurers came by land.

The maritime fur traders did not establish permanent settlements in the Pacific Northwest. They came and went, conducting their business, but they had little or no interest in the land itself. When the fur trade era died, the Pacific Northwest might have reverted back to unvisited wilderness had it not been for the genesis of land-based explorations. A few ships were still carrying furs to China when men began coming overland from the interior of North America. They were harbingers of the immigrants who came later to make permanent homes and who would change the land and its people.

After the War of 1812, a dispute arose over the "Oregon country." England and the United States signed a "treaty of joint occupation" in 1818, and for several decades they shared dual custody, each keeping a wary eye on the other. During this period Yankee settlers mingled with the Hudson's Bay Company's fur traders. The company established Fort Nisqually on Puget Sound in 1833. Meanwhile, the United States negotiated a treaty with Spain and another with Russia which effectively removed those nations from the struggle for control of the territory between the Columbia River and latitude 54° 40' north and extending from the Pacific Ocean to the Rocky Mountains. Although the coastline of this area had been explored by 1803, virtually nothing was known about the interior.

The fact that England and the United States both occupied Oregon did not prevent each country from attempting to obtain permanent jurisdiction. England coveted the Puget Sound region, but so did the United States, and at one point England offered its opponent the entire Olympic Peninsula—everything north of a line drawn from Grays Harbor to Hood Canal—if the Americans would agree to accept the Columbia River as the boundary between Canada and the United States. The peninsula was thus used as a pawn at the bargaining table. However, the United States refused the offer.

About the time the mariners were leaving the scene, the Lewis and Clark Expedition called attention to the Oregon country. Four decades later, the United States reinforced its claim to the Pacific Northwest when the Wilkes Expedition, commanded by Lieutenant Charles Wilkes, U.S.N., included in its survey a detailed investigation of Puget Sound in 1841. The expedition also dispatched land parties and named geographic features.

With the seafarers gone, but England and the United States still quarreling over the territory, a vanguard (comprised of hunters, trappers, traders, adventurers, explorers, missionaries, and others) was attracted to the region, to be quickly overtaken during the 1840s and 1850s by a flood of land-hungry emigrants caught up with "Oregon fever" who were anxious to reach the land where roses bloomed at Christmas. The latter traveled westward via the Oregon Trail to the lower Columbia. Most of them

A homestead on the lower Elwha (Photo courtesy National Park Service)

settled in the Willamette Valley, south of the Columbia, but some went north from Fort Vancouver to the Puget Sound country. Gradually, however, the numbers migrating north increased.

The first settlements on the Olympic Peninsula by non-Indians occurred at this time, primarily on the northern and eastern fringes, where the land was partially shielded by the mountains from winter storms. This settlement, like that elsewhere in the Puget Sound country, was usually close to salt water, because the dense forests were inhospitable, trails few, and roads almost nonexistent. People traveled via the waterways whenever possible, and any place not close to the sea or a navigable stream was considered to be remote.

The first to settle at the head of Puget Sound was Michael T. Simmons, the Pacific Northwest's equivalent of Daniel Boone. He defied the Hudson's Bay Company in 1845 by leading a little band of Americans to the Sound, thus extending the Oregon Trail northward. He also founded the town of New Market, or Tumwater, the first American community established on Puget Sound. This action helped break the monopoly held by the Hudson's Bay Company's fur traders. In 1853 Simmons erected the first sawmills on the Olympic Peninsula, near the head of Puget Sound. He built a water-driven mill on a stream that flowed into Big Skookum Inlet, but a flood destroyed it. He constructed a replacement, only to see it suffer the same fate. Simmons later abandoned the mill business and became an Indian agent.

While the overland migrations were occurring during the first half of the nineteenth century, the Olympic Peninsula remained an isolated, unsought corner, a land wild, remote, and untraveled. But it was not unclaimed. Gradually the scales of settlement were tipped, however, in favor of the United States by the increasing numbers of Americans, like Simmons, who chose to live in the Puget Sound basin. After much wrangling and negotiation, the boundary between Canada and the United States was fixed in 1846 at the forty-ninth parallel of latitude, except that it dipped down to the Strait of Juan de Fuca so that England could retain all of Vancouver Island.

This action opened the door to widespread settlement on the peninsula. Nevertheless, the dense forests, paucity of land suitable for agriculture, and rugged terrain repelled rather than beckoned settlers. Initially, most of them ended up on the shores of Hood Canal and the Strait of Juan de Fuca, because these were the most hospitable areas. The Pacific coast—remote, rain-drenched, and uninviting—was ignored for years, and the heavily timbered southern slope was virtually inaccessible.

Oregon Territory, created by the United States in 1848, embraced most of the Pacific Northwest. Two years later the office of Surveyor General of Public Lands in Oregon came into being. This happened because of the great interest in the public domain, and it provided for surveying and donation land claims. As a result, Americans were now greedily looking over the territory England had relinquished. The United States purchased the Hudson's Bay Company's interests in Oregon Territory, and the company moved to Victoria, B.C., on Vancouver Island.

The company then sent trappers into the northern Olympics in quest of fur-bearing animals. These men were the first non-Indians to penetrate the Olympic Mountains to any great distance. Two of them, John Sutherland and John Everett, paddled across the Strait of Juan de Fuca in a dugout canoe and visited with Clallam Indians before going into the mountains. The Indians told them about two large lakes in the foothills that were haunted by spirits, and indicated they seldom visited the lakes because they heard eerie sounds made by ghosts. This did not deter Everett and Sutherland, who were probably the first white men to see the lakes. They set traps along the shores, and concluded while doing so that the weird noises the Indians heard were the sounds made by two large fir trees rubbing against each other when the wind blew hard. The men named the lakes for themselves. The smaller, slipper-shaped one (called Naketa by the Indians) they named Lake Sutherland; the larger one (later renamed Lake Crescent) became Lake Everett.

Everett and Sutherland decided to remain in Washington, and they became well-known pioneers on the peninsula. They continued to roam the Olympics and were among the vanguard of "mountain men"—the itinerant hunters, trappers, fishermen, and prospectors who filtered into the foothills. Everett was perhaps the prototype of that breed of wanderer. He ranged the Olympics widely, often for weeks at a time, packing a blanket or two, a gun and ammunition, a meager supply of provisions, and a small sack of salt.

Because resolution of the dispute between England and the United States stimulated rapid settlement of the Puget Sound country, several towns were founded in the early 1850s. One of them, Olympia, at the head of the Sound, later became the capital of Washington Territory. Other communities included Seattle and Steilacoom. On the Olympic Peninsula, Port Townsend was founded in 1851, and the general belief was that it was destined to become the chief seaport of the Pacific Northwest; however, that honor went to Seattle instead. The first settlers at New Dungeness also arrived in 1851. The region's growth was rapid; but, by today's standards, this vast area was essentially empty, with much land yet available to homestead. The settlers on Puget Sound and the Olympic Peninsula were few in number, and they were isolated from Salem, the capital of Oregon Territory, by miles of trackless old-growth forest and the unbridged Columbia River. Consequently, the people living north of the river quickly petitioned Congress to divide Oregon by creating a new territory bounded by the Columbia on the south. Washington Territory thus came into being in 1853, Olympia was designated the capital, and Isaac I. Stevens was appointed governor. At this time, whites living north of the Columbia numbered fewer than four thousand persons.

Up to this time the newcomers of European ancestry who had settled in the region had not suddenly taken over the land. Accordingly, the Indians had tolerated the whites who at first came in small numbers—the trappers, traders, and Hudson's Bay Company men. Eventually, they came as settlers also, but still they were few in number. Over a period of years the Indians had become accustomed to co-existing with whites who did not outnumber them. But the white population slowly, gradually increased, settlement accelerated, and not until they were, in fact, outnumbered did the Indians realize they were losing their land. But by then it was too late. They had been demoralized by the white man's liquor and diseases, their spirits crushed, and their traditional ways of life disrupted. Then, shortly after Washington Territory was created, the Indian campfires were rekindled and flared briefly: the Indians rebelled and attempted to drive the whites away. However, Governor Stevens, who was also Superintendent of Indian Affairs, called them to council. As a result, treaties were signed whereby the Indians relinquished most of their lands, but they received little in return. The treaties with the Indians on the Olympic Peninsula—signed in 1855 and 1856—resulted in their ceding to the United States the entire peninsula except for portions set aside as reservations.

Meanwhile, a United States Coast Survey party headed by Lieutenant George Davidson arrived at Cape Flattery in 1852. This party had been surveying the Pacific coast area since 1850, to meet the needs of navigation, and its duties included not only determining the exact locations of the chief harbors but also establishing lines of latitude and longitude.

Other than Mount Olympus, none of the peninsula's mountains had been distinguished with a name. This omission was corrected to some extent in 1856 when Davidson, then engaged in surveying Puget Sound, named several prominent peaks that were visible from that body of water: petite Mount Ellinor, for his sweetheart, Ellinor Fauntleroy, whom he married in 1858; bosomy Mount Constance, after her sister; and The Brothers, a conspicuous, double-peaked mountain, in honor of their brothers, Edward and Arthur Fauntleroy.

Naming peaks was not exploring them, however, and the Olympics remained unknown except for what could be learned from a distance. Settlers were working hard to establish homes by busily clearing plots in the virgin forests. Most were unable to spare the time needed to explore the country, but a handful did manage to prowl the mountains and ascend the higher peaks.

Or so it was claimed. According to various assertions, during the 1850s the summit snows of several Northwest mountains—Mount St. Helens, Mount Adams, and Mount Olympus—first felt the imprint of calked boots, and an Army officer climbed high on the flanks of Mount Rainier. Mount St. Helens and Mount Adams may have yielded to conquest at this time, but the alleged first ascent of Mount Olympus in 1854 is probably spurious, the "facts" regarding the climb having gone unreported for more than fifty years. Two of the alleged climbers, Michael T. Simmons and Benjamin F. Shaw, were also said to have crossed the Olympics from Lake Cushman to Quinault Lake—that is, from east to west—about this time, but this tale lacks verification as well. More than likely, the journey never happened. The contention was also made that, in the company of two other men, Simmons and Shaw made the "first partial ascent of Mount Rainier."

The Olympic Mountains remained *terra incognita,* an unknown and mysterious land, because they still had not been explored nearly a century after Meares named Mount Olympus. The reason they had not been explored was that, surrounded as they were by dense, impenetrable forests, the rugged peaks were so difficult of access that explorers were simply unwilling to face the necessary hardships. But while the mountains slept, undisturbed by man, cities like Seattle and Tacoma were growing up almost within the shadows cast by the peaks. On clear days their residents could see the snow-covered heights, but no one had walked upon them.

Although government maps at that time were reasonably accurate in their depiction of the Olympic Peninsula's coastline, they were blank with respect to the interior. Consequently it was believed that the streams that flowed from the mountains rose on the outward slopes. This led to speculation as to what lay behind the first ranges. Was there, as various legends indicated, a large basin or valley which contained a huge lake that had a subterranean outlet? Was this central valley inhabited by fierce cannibals, and did this explain why the coastal Indians were reluctant to go into the interior? Or did vast expanses of rolling prairies, alive with game, lie between the inner slopes and the big lake? Most important of all, did the Olympics harbor rich deposits of minerals that awaited discovery by prospectors, or was the unexplored region merely a timberland?

The questions cried out for answers. The stage was therefore set, during the closing days of the American frontier, for exploration of the Olympic Mountains.

2

The First Expeditions

EXCEPT FOR THE INDIANS, WHO MADE occasional, unrecorded visits, the first adventurers who actually set foot in the Olympic Mountains and did not "explore" them from afar were the so-called "mountain men," who began wandering through the trackless forests in the 1850s. If the homesteaders on the peninsula's shores had little time to explore, the "mountain men" were free to come and go wherever and whenever they wished. They did not organize "expeditions," and usually went alone or with two or three companions. They did not build trails, and they seldom wrote about their adventures.

The "mountain men" were itinerant hunters, trappers, prospectors, and fishermen. They traveled great distances, sometimes for weeks or months, packing blankets, guns, ammunition, flour, salt, and perhaps a bit of sourdough starter. During their wanderings, many of them climbed the less challenging peaks merely to look around. The newspapers sometimes took note, briefly, of their activities, but these accounts were usually not reliable. When asked to tell their stories, the prospectors often spun exaggerated tales, at times claiming discovery of minerals where none existed. On occasion they said the country was rougher than it was; at other times they said just the opposite. But the fishermen were worse: every "hole" had from twenty to a hundred trout, and the fish attained incredible size and weight.

The "mountain men" came and went their solitary ways, but about thirty years after their arrival, the speculation voiced about the Olympics began to yield results. In 1878 the so-called Watkinson Expedition crossed the southern fringes of the Olympics. This was not a formal, organized expedition, but it was more than just unplanned wandering. Eldridge Morse, who wrote about the journey two years later, claimed this was "the only trip ever made by white men from Hood Canal to the Ocean, over the top of the Olympic Mountains." According to Morse, the Indians never crossed the mountains, they always went around them. And one will note, when marking the Watkinson Expedition's route on a map, that the men did not actually traverse the mountains from one side to the other, as did the later Press Expedition, but cut an arc across a large chunk of the periphery. Still, it was a notable achievement. The party, consisting of five young loggers, was led by Melbourne Watkinson, the Mason County sheriff's son. The others were Finley McRae, George McLaughlin, Benjamin Armstrong, and Charles Armstrong. The men knew nothing about mineralogy, but they made the trip because gold had been found on Hood Canal. They were, however, skilled hunters and anglers, and supplemented their menu with grouse, elk, deer, fish, huckle-berries, and salmonberries.

The men left the sheriff's house at Lilliwaup Creek, with the officer's dog in their company, on September 2, 1878. They walked to Lake Cushman, then proceeded several miles up the North Fork Skokomish before leaving the river to climb over the divide. On September 5, late in the afternoon, they got to the top of a mountain they estimated was "about as high as Mount Olympus and nearly due west of it." This it could not have been, because they were nowhere near Olympus, and certainly not west of it. The peak they climbed was on the divide between streams flowing east and west, and they estimated the snow depth on the top to be thirty-five feet.

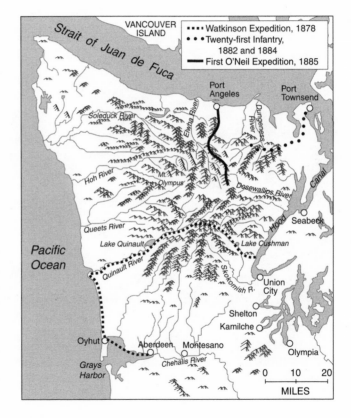

Port Townsend, Washington, in the 1890s (Photo courtesy the Collection of the Jefferson County Historical Society, Port Townsend, Washington)

The exact place where the men crossed the divide is unknown because Morse's account is vague, but it must have been somewhere between Six Ridge Pass and O'Neil Pass. When they did cross over, their dog—who had more sense than they—deserted them and went home. The men traveled down either Graves Creek or O'Neil Creek to the East Fork Quinault, then followed the river to Quinault Lake, where they came upon a band of Indians who took them downriver to the ocean. They then walked the beach to Grays Harbor, arriving on September 14. The men returned home by way of the Chehalis River valley and Union City. Their trek had lasted eighteen days.

Less than four years later, the United States Army initiated the first organized attempt to explore the Olympic Mountains and build a trail. This was undertaken by units of the Twenty-first Infantry stationed at Fort Townsend, Washington Territory, a military post on the northeastern tip of the peninsula. On May 22, 1882, Lieutenant Colonel Alexander Chambers dispatched Lieutenant Willis Wittich, Company B, into the district lying back of the fort. His task was to reconnoiter a route and cut a trail between the fort and the Dungeness River. He was accompanied by a civilian packer, a pack train, and five enlisted men.

After hacking a way through the dense undergrowth for two weeks, Wittich returned to the fort on June 5. But he left again five days later "to complete the instructions contained in Post Order 47." His party returned to the post on July 13. A week later, First Lieutenant Thomas H. Bradley, Company D, left to extend the trail. He had under his charge a civilian packer, a pack train, and several enlisted men from his company.

Several weeks later, Colonel Chambers joined Bradley's party to personally direct the work. Accompanied by John M. Kollock, a contract surgeon, he left Fort Townsend on August 25 to explore the mountains "in compliance with verbal instructions from the Department Commander." The doctor provided medical service for the party. Chambers was absent from the post until September 17, and Kollock returned to Fort Townsend with Bradley's party on September 23. From time to time other enlisted men were added to the work force.

This military expedition had been well organized and it had attacked the Olympics with considerable energy. After six months of difficult labor, the troopers had succeeded in cutting to and across both branches of the Dungeness River. However, upon reaching the last range of foothills, the soldiers considered the way too difficult, and they abandoned the project. In November, a sergeant was dispatched to make a "final inspection" of the trail.

The Army did nothing more to explore the Olympics until the spring of 1884, when another Twenty-first Infantry work party, under charge of Second Lieutenants Charles M. Truitt,

Enlisted men's barracks, Fort Townsend (Photo courtesy the Collection of the Jefferson County Historical Society, Port Townsend, Washington)

Company D, and Willson Y. Stamper, Company B, attempted to reopen the trail that had been started by Wittich and Bradley. This party was absent from the post from May 17 to 26, "surveying trail to Snowy Range," as the Army aptly designated the Olympics. In addition to the officers, the party included four enlisted men.

Because the United States Army's attempts to explore the Olympic Mountains in the early 1880s had met with only rudimentary success, the opportunity to unlock the country's secrets was still present. Apparently, fate selected Lieutenant Joseph P. O'Neil, Company B, Fourteenth Infantry, to do the job. On June 25, 1884—two years after the preliminary attempts by Wittich and Bradley—a battalion of the Fourteenth Infantry that included Company B left Fort Sidney, Nebraska, and traveled by rail and steamship to the Pacific Northwest. The battalion arrived at Fort Townsend on July 8.

Lieutenant O'Neil was twenty-one years old, and had graduated with honors from the University of Notre Dame in 1883, receiving a Bachelor of Science degree. He had been commissioned a second lieutenant on February 4, 1884, and assigned to Company B, Fourteenth Infantry, which was stationed at Fort Sidney. Shortly after he arrived in the Pacific Northwest, O'Neil became the Signal and Engineer Officer at Fort Townsend. He served in that capacity until April 29, 1885, when his company was transferred to Vancouver Barracks, Washington Territory, about 175 miles due south.

O'Neil had been interested in the Olympics when stationed at Fort Townsend, but he was doubly inspired to explore them when he sailed up Puget Sound during the journey to Vancouver Barracks. The snow-draped mountains shone forth in all their splendor on the bright spring day, and the lieutenant admired, with "youthful enthusiasm," the rugged peaks. He was practical enough to note, however, that their "boldness and abruptness" appeared to stand as an "impenetrable barrier to the farther advance of man and civilization." He thereupon resolved to explore the region at the first opportunity.

During the year O'Neil had been stationed at Fort Townsend, he had not been able to go into the Olympics, but he had inquired about the region. Because the Twenty-first Infantry had left the Pacific Northwest for the Department of the Platte before O'Neil arrived at the fort, he had not had an opportunity to speak to the men who had worked on the trail, with the possible exception of Lieutenant Wittich and three enlisted men who had remained at the post on detached service until July 18. O'Neil did direct inquiries to the settlers who lived near the fort, but he received conflicting reports as to the nature of the country. He was told that the mountains enclosed vast prairies, and that one could pole a canoe up the Elwha River, cross over the divide, and float down another river to the Pacific Ocean. However, due to what he regarded as a paucity of reliable information, he concluded that the Olympics were as wild as Alaska, with actual knowledge about them limited to the perimeter. He noted that the Indians never went beyond the foothills, and that only a few trappers, hunters, and prospectors had been bold enough to go beyond the outer barriers. O'Neil understood why: the steep ridges, the dense forests, and the tangled undergrowth presented difficult problems in slashing a trail into the interior.

Shortly after he arrived at Vancouver Barracks, O'Neil prevailed upon General Nelson A. Miles, the department commander, to let him lead an expedition into the Olympics. Miles had been inclined to discredit the "wonderful stories" that were told about the region, but he was surprised that in such a prosperous country "so much seemingly valuable territory should be unknown." He therefore agreed to dispatch an exploring party with O'Neil in command.

The trip was formally authorized on July 6, 1885. O'Neil's orders directed him to reconnoiter the Olympic Mountains, and they specified that he would be provided with a detail of three enlisted men, plus several pack mules to provide transportation. Because the summer was well under way, O'Neil put the expedition together quickly. The party of six men and several pack mules left Vancouver Barracks two days later. The personnel consisted of Lieutenant O'Neil, Sergeant Richard D. Green, Sergeant Henry C. Weagraff, and Private John Johnson, plus two civilian engineers, Harry Hawgood and Richard Habersham. At least two of the six had prior experience in mountains. Weagraff had accompanied a Signal Corps party to Mount Hood in 1884, and Johnson, while serving in the Twenty-first Infantry, had helped build the "Snowy Range" trail from Fort Townsend to the Dungeness River.

When the time came to decide where to begin exploring, the men hesitated. The Olympics appeared to be a jumble of peaks with no obvious route to the interior. However, because of the nearness of Port Angeles to the mountains, the men selected the little community as their base of operations. Accordingly, on July 16, the expedition proceeded by steamer from Port Townsend down the Strait of Juan de Fuca, and arrived in Port Angeles that evening. The village had about forty inhabitants, and everyone turned out to help. The animals were pastured, the equipment and supplies placed in storage. The explorers set up headquarters in the local hotel, where they conferred with the townsfolk about the best way to approach the mountains. One of the most vocal men was Norman R. Smith, whose father had been one of the town's founders. Smith told O'Neil that he had lived on the peninsula for years. He was, in fact, destined to become the second mayor of Port Angeles six years later. He was a promoter who favored development of the country, and he believed that eventually a railroad would be built northward from Grays Harbor to the Quillayute country, and thence eastward to Port Angeles. When Smith volunteered to join the expedition, O'Neil readily agreed to accept his services.

According to Smith, the "Olympic Range" formed a V, with its apex near the upper reaches of Hood Canal, the long, narrow inlet bordering the peninsula on the east. One side of this V ran north, paralleling Hood Canal, and included the peaks visible from Puget Sound. The other side extended northwesterly to Mount Olympus, ending in foothills near Cape Flattery.

The men considered, then planned a tentative route up the Elwha, which appeared to head near the center of the Olympics. The party would leave the mountains by going down the Quinault River to the ocean.

The expedition left Port Angeles on Friday, July 17, and headed for the mountains to the south. At first the men followed the right-of-way the settlers had partially cleared for the county road, then utilized an old trail once used by Indians to pack game from the foothills. Working side by side, soldiers and settlers spent the day stumbling through underbrush and cutting out logs, and

Lieutenant Joseph P. O'Neil, Fourteenth Infantry, circa 1890 (Photo courtesy Robert B. Hitchman)

they progressed "perhaps a mile in an hour and a half." Blocked at times by windfalls, they arrived in late afternoon at an almost impassable marsh, where one mule got mired in the swamp. At this point, where the old trail disappeared, the expedition was forced to camp. Much fatigued as they were, the men slept soundly, although during the night the scream of a prowling cougar almost caused the mules to stampede.

The foothills were now less than five miles distant. The next day Hawgood and Smith set out to locate a trail route, while O'Neil climbed a knoll to get first-hand knowledge of the country. Hawgood reported the terrain ahead would be difficult to traverse because cliffs, precipices, and windfalls barred the way. O'Neil therefore revised his plans. The settlers again attempted to be helpful and offered free advice. One man, Frank Chambers, Sr., suggested the expedition follow Yennis Creek instead of the Elwha. After discussing the matter, O'Neil decided to take his advice and shift the line of march toward the peak known today as Mount Angeles.

O'Neil's plan called for scouts to precede the main party in order to prospect a route and map trails. After he selected the most promising way, the trail cutters were to clear the path, with the pack train operating in the rear, relaying supplies from camp to camp. He anticipated the expedition would proceed southeasterly until it struck the head of the Dungeness, then turn south and travel along the divide bounded on the west by the Elwha and Quinault, on the east by the Dosewallips and Duckabush. This would make it possible to explore the interior, and he would send his scouts out in various directions. When the explorations concluded, the party would descend via the Quinault and then follow the coast to Grays Harbor.

Although they had had a taste of what to expect, the men did not as yet appreciate the difficulties ahead. They soon discovered, however, that while they might progress five or six miles on certain days, on others they were unable to advance more than a quarter of a mile. They worked long hours. Breakfast was eaten at five a.m. and an hour later they were busy cutting a trail. Except for lunch, the men worked steadily all day, had supper at six p.m., then retired.

The expedition moved to a small tributary of Yennis Creek on July 21, and, when clearing a campsite, the men dug up a well-preserved human skull. Of course, they could not do otherwise than name the stream Skull Creek. The hills were getting steeper, and this was emphasized a day or so later when two mules lost their footing and rolled into the creek. O'Neil thought they had been killed, "but the packer, with the assistance of one of the men and a large amount of profanity, succeeded in releasing their packs." The animals then stood up and began grazing as if nothing had happened. O'Neil remarked that he had had "many occasions to notice that the gift of volubility in strong, terse and emphatic language is a special gift of men accustomed to handling mules." The next day another mule rolled down the hill, but it was less fortunate; the animal was so badly injured they were forced to abandon it.

The men had now cleared the trail almost to the base of the first range of snow-clad peaks. During this part of the trip, through the foothills of the Olympics, game had been scarce, and the explorers had had poor luck hunting; consequently, they had been dependent upon their government rations. They had, in fact, tasted fresh meat only once since they left Port Angeles. O'Neil attributed the lack of wildlife to the unavoidable noise made by the trail builders. Although the expedition's supply of pork, bacon, flour, beans, and coffee sustained them, the men desired fresh meat on occasion. By late July, their provisions were beginning to run low, and the men were almost fasting, with the hard work beginning to tell upon their health. However, after spending a week cutting a trail through the foothills, the expedition was ready to move into the high country and make a base camp on the first range. Once this was accomplished, the men could explore in various directions. If feasible, O'Neil would follow the

Mount Anderson from Hayden Pass Trail (Photo by Frank O. Shaw)

plan previously outlined—cross the mountains to the Pacific slope, then travel to Grays Harbor and return to Fort Townsend by steamship.

On Sunday, July 27, O'Neil and Smith set out to prospect a route ahead. They followed an elk trail about six miles, and this led them into a little valley surrounded by lofty peaks, with sheer cliffs rising abruptly on all sides. The mountains adjacent to this valley appeared to be a range that paralleled the Strait of Juan de Fuca. Capping the ridge at the valley's head were two mountains that O'Neil called the Sister Peaks. Between them was a gap the men named Victor Pass, after Smith's father, the late Victor J. Smith. O'Neil and Smith then climbed to the pass and ascended a ridge to make observations. Here they discovered that the Sister Peaks gave them their "first good view of the Olympics, exterior and interior."

The Strait lay far below, to the north; but looking to the east, west, and south, the men could see snow-clad peaks rising in "wild, broken confusion" above deep, forested valleys. The lieutenant noted that the Olympics had "no regularity about their formation," but they appeared to be "jumbled up in the utmost confusion." The only regularity he could detect was that the ranges nearest to the Strait and Puget Sound appeared to run parallel to those bodies of salt water. O'Neil thought Mount Olympus was the "grandest sight." This cluster of icy peaks and pinnacles appeared to be the center of a range which had no pronounced direction, but seemed to circle on itself, paralleled on its outer course by the Elwha. The lieutenant had neither met nor heard of anyone who had been near Olympus, and he therefore resolved to tackle its mysteries. He decided that after the expedition crossed Victor Pass and reached the second range, he would divide the party. He would lead the main group to the southeast, while Hawgood took charge of the other and traced the Elwha to its headwaters.

When O'Neil and Smith came upon a band of elk, Smith killed a yearling. Elated, the men camped where they were and quickly prepared their evening meal. After dining on fresh elk steak, they "felt more in the humor for traveling," and they kept going until darkness made it too dangerous to go on. When they spotted a wolf prowling in the twilight, they used the animal for target practice, and Smith succeeded in crippling it. O'Neil supposed that many predators roamed the Olympics, but this was the only wolf he saw during the party's stay in the mountains. That night the men slept in a deserted bear's den to escape the cold.

The next morning O'Neil and Smith followed the ridge until they could overlook the Elwha. The lieutenant now discovered, to his chagrin, that he should have disregarded the advice he had received from Frank Chambers. Had he approached the

Olympics from some place between Port Angeles and the Elwha, as originally planned, the expedition could have gotten into the interior "with much less trail cutting and fewer steep hills to climb." However, the party had gone too far now to turn back and search elsewhere for another route. Within two or three days the expedition would be in the high, parklike meadows where travel would be less difficult.

During their reconnaissance, O'Neil and Smith discovered, to their surprise, many traces of hunters. Apparently, this northern slope of the Olympics was better known than legend and tradition had indicated. In fact, the men stumbled upon an old log cabin that hunting parties had used. The wildness of the game plainly indicated that the animals had been shot at before, and was further proof that hunters had been on this range.

O'Neil and Smith then retraced their steps, crossed Victor Pass shortly after sunset, and hurried down the mountain, reaching the expedition's camp long after dark. The next day they set out for Port Angeles, taking with them the two crippled mules. The men then hired an Indian guide, who accompanied them as they made their way back to the expedition's camp. As they did so, they could see that a fire was raging in the foothills.

Sergeant Richard D. Green, Fourteenth Infantry (Photo courtesy Zeno Berry)

This induced them to quicken their pace because they feared the fire would cross the trail and prevent their reaching camp. They arrived safely after dark, but almost got shot by their own men, who had been on the alert because a notorious outlaw was said to be in the vicinity and because a cougar was prowling on the camp's outskirts.

O'Neil had hired the Indian to guide them over an old, indistinct trail. But the excitement brought on by the combination of fire, cougar, and outlaw proved too much. When the guide saw where the explorers were camped and realized where they were headed, neither the promise of big pay nor the threat of death detained him, and during the night he disappeared. O'Neil blamed it on the fear and superstition of the Indians that their god, the Thunderbird, would inflict terrible vengeance upon those who, by entering, desecrated its abode. However, O'Neil was neither intimidated by the legend nor deterred by the tangible physical obstacles. The explorers returned to work, hacked a path along Yennis Creek, and by early August had completed the trail to the base of the Miles Range, the name O'Neil gave to the peaks and ridges paralleling the Strait. They marked the way so clearly that a novice could traverse, in a day or two, terrain the expedition had taken nearly three weeks to carve a route through. O'Neil now moved the expedition's camp to the little valley nestled in the Miles Range. Here the men first saw Olympic marmots; after killing one,

they shot no more because they found it "pleasant when traveling through the wilds to hear their cheerful call."

The steep terrain at the valley's head made it difficult to cut a trail over Victor Pass, but they solved the engineering problems. They did not have to descend much on the south side of the first range; therefore they reached the second range more easily than they had the first range. Nevertheless, when they moved the expedition's camp across the pass, several mules rolled down the precipitous slope, and only after the "expenditure of much time, energy, and language" were the men able to get the animals back on the trail.

Upon moving to the second range, O'Neil set up the expedition's "main cache camp" on a prominent point which had a good view of the numerous ranges. The men were now ready to explore, and they planned their itinerary from the tent. O'Neil estimated they were perhaps twelve miles from the Elwha, but several steep ridges lay between them and the river.

The lieutenant divided the expedition. He directed Hawgood to take one division and proceed to the Elwha, follow the stream to its head, and come out somewhere on the southwest slope of the Olympics. Meanwhile, O'Neil would lead the other division to the southeast, locate the head of the Elwha's East Fork, then make his way to Hood Canal.

Hawgood's party traveled about a week, until it became

impossible to proceed with a pack train. The engineer had almost decided to abandon the mules and have the men backpack everything up the Elwha when an accident occurred that abruptly ended the activities of this group. The party had just crossed the East Fork; the pack animals were climbing the far side, when a mule slipped and came near to causing the loss of the whole pack train. Another mule rolled from the trail, its pack loosened, and the detachment's provisions, mess outfit, and instruments tumbled into the river and could not be retrieved. The mule rolled some distance, then trees broke its fall. The men succeeded in getting it to camp, and it was later taken to a farm near Port Angeles.

The disaster left Hawgood's men "hungry, tired and discouraged." Unable to continue, they returned to the main camp to await O'Neil's division, evidently having concluded that the lieutenant could not proceed to Hood Canal as planned.

Meanwhile, the unit led by O'Neil followed the ridge leading southeasterly from the main camp. At times travel was comparatively easy, but the terrain was "often broken by sharp peaks." The subalpine meadows nourished luxuriant grasses, and the mules, who had become "worn and thin by constant travel," now began to gain weight, despite being subjected to much strenuous up-and-down activity. The lieutenant's division kept to the ridges and descended into the valleys, where water was available,

only when it had to find campsites. The country near the timberline was quite picturesque, dotted as it was with little tarns and clusters of subalpine trees.

The explorers "never wanted for fresh meat" from this point on. In fact, the men saw an elk herd almost daily. O'Neil did not allow anyone to shoot an elk without special permission, and this was given only when the group needed meat. He then detailed one man to supply the camp with elk, deer, bear, and game birds—and even this huntsman could not kill when the larder was stocked. The abundance of game could be attributed—at least in part—to the fact that the explorers were now going through country where the animals had never been hunted.

As the expedition moved deeper into the mountains, the topographic configuration of the ridges turned it to a southerly direction. The route now followed the divide between streams flowing north and west, on the one hand, and to the east, on the other. Several miles beyond Noplace—the name the men gave their last camp, the point where they abandoned trail building—another peak barred the way, with the descent everywhere so precipitous that taking the mules down its sides was impractical. O'Neil therefore decided to leave the animals at Noplace while the men explored on foot.

He resolved to tramp without the mules until he could find

a place to get them across, or discover the source of the East Fork of the Elwha. Accompanied by Private Johnson and a civilian camp follower, he went ahead to look for a route. Carrying forty-pound packs, the trio traveled south, through the heart of the Olympics. O'Neil was favorably impressed by the scenery—the timbered vales, canyons, waterfalls, and "snow-topped mountains." Often they passed "large fields of ice and snow . . . and trees dotting a landscape of green in the valleys."

The men tramped for eleven hours the first day, then slept that night in a deserted bear's den. They could now see what the lieutenant took to be the source of the East Fork "and the field of ice from which it started."

The scouts traveled southward for several more days and observed numerous bands of elk and much small game. The animals were so tame that hunting them was like shooting domestic cattle—merely a matter of selecting the animal desired and killing it. When traveling through the valleys, the men frequently came upon what O'Neil called "elk yards," places he took to be the winter home of the elk. At times the yards covered hundreds of acres; they were invariably located on the southern slope of a ridge or peak, but so hemmed in by the forest and terrain as to be

The Olympics from Hurricane Ridge (Photo by Frank O. Shaw)

protected on every side. Within the elk yards, the trees were denuded of their bark, the bushes cut down, and the ground severely trampled.

The civilian quickly tired of the strenuous tramping. He deserted O'Neil and Johnson and returned to Noplace, but O'Neil was too excited by the changing vistas to consider turning back, and Johnson loyally tagged along. The two traveled for several days along the ridge that overlooked the East Fork. They did not attempt to descend to the stream, but were content to look down into the valley and its side canyons. O'Neil and Johnson circled around the ice field at the stream's head, then struck out toward a peak the lieutenant wished to climb to take observations. They made the ascent with some difficulty, but were rewarded by an outstanding view from the summit. They could see the volcanic cones of the Cascades, and they were surrounded by the peaks of the Olympics.

When they retraced the route to their last camp, the men again came to the snowfield which was the source of the East Fork. Here, contrary to his better judgment, O'Neil yielded to impulse and, instead of following the longer ridge route, descended the snowfield. The snow was hard and slippery, the incline steep. Halfway down, O'Neil had to leap a crevasse ten feet wide. Upon completing the jump, he lost his balance, fell, and slid rapidly down the snowfield, coming to a stop at its base. He signaled for

Johnson not to follow him, but to return via the ridge. Johnson was much excited by the mishap, and in trying to reach O'Neil quickly, he took a shortcut, became bewildered by the ravines, and wandered away, lost.

When Johnson failed to appear, O'Neil slowly made his way back to their camp, thinking he would find his companion there, but the place was deserted. The lieutenant then built several large fires "on all the points around" to indicate the camp's location, but Johnson still did not appear. After wandering around and firing his gun to attract attention, O'Neil headed for Noplace, with the hope of better luck, but again he was disappointed.

The lieutenant sent everyone out to look for the missing man, but, after several days of fruitless search, he concluded Johnson's "only chance of safety lay in his own judgment." O'Neil then took his division back to the main cache camp, where he found Hawgood's party. Once again everyone was sent out to look for Johnson, but to no avail.

The men were gathered around the campfire, working on a map, when a messenger arrived from Department Headquarters. The courier presented O'Neil with orders from the Adjutant General's Office directing that he report on September 1 to the Infantry and Cavalry School at Fort Leavenworth, Kansas. This meant he would have to abandon the explorations shortly, but he delayed his departure as long as possible; then,

leaving Sergeant Weagraff in charge to continue the search for Johnson, he returned to Vancouver Barracks. He left that post on August 26, en route to Fort Leavenworth.

O'Neil regretted leaving, not only because Johnson was still missing but also because his reconnaissance was incomplete. He realized, however, that the favorable season for exploring was now about over, but lurking in the back of his mind was the thought that he would return at some future date and finish his explorations.

When he lost contact with O'Neil, Johnson realized he was lost. Apparently, he headed northeast in hopes of striking the "Snowy Range" trail which he had helped build in 1882. He wandered around for six days, subsisting on wild berries, then reached a small settlement and notified the military authorities of his whereabouts. He arrived at Fort Townsend on August 25, where he waited until the other members of the expedition returned. On September 7, he was sent, together with the rest of the party, to Vancouver Barracks.

O'Neil wrote to the Assistant Adjutant General at Vancouver Barracks on November 19, enclosing a copy of his report of the reconnaissance made and a map of the district explored. He pointed out that his little expedition had been in the Olympics six weeks, from July 17 to August 26. Although the travel was difficult, he felt that the adventure, the picturesque scenery, and the splendid hunting and fishing amply compensated for the hardships. He regretted he had had to leave before completing the planned work, and he felt certain he could have accomplished his purpose had more time been available. He also stated he had no special objects in mind—all he wished to learn was "the character of the country and its topography."

"The country remained a *terra incognita* until 1885," O'Neil later wrote, "when General Miles ordered me to make an attempt to explore it. . . . Up to '85 no one could say what the country was, but when I came out of it that year I knew it was the last home of the elk. The dense forests and denser undergrowth around the base of these mountains extending about twenty miles back from the water render all attempts to enter, but the most systematic trail cutting, abortive. The rivers can not be ascended to the interior of the mountains on account of the swiftness of the current and the numerous impassable falls, and it is [owing] to this that some portions of these mountains are alive with game having no fear of man."

O'Neil had performed a valuable service. His reconnaissance paved the way for further exploration, including his own more ambitious 1890 expedition. The trail built by his men led from Port Angeles in a southeasterly direction, then southward to Noplace, "in the heart of the mountains." The trail was used by hunters, fishermen, and prospectors for years. Most of the area traversed was included in the Olympic Forest Reserve in 1897. During the 1930s the government built a road along part of the route; then, after the creation of Olympic National Park, the National Park Service constructed a modern highway that more or less follows O'Neil's path from Port Angeles to the general area of the expedition's "main cache camp" on Hurricane Ridge.

Although the lieutenant's 1885 expedition did not succeed in crossing the Olympics, it kindled interest in plans for other expeditions. O'Neil's party had made a good beginning, and it was followed, less than five years later, by a more spectacular operation, the Press Expedition, and by a little-publicized father-and-son team, the Gilmans.

3

Gilman and Banta Explorations

LESS THAN A MONTH BEFORE WASH-
ington Territory achieved statehood in the autumn
of 1889, a pair of newcomers set forth on the first
of two extended treks on the Olympic Peninsula.
Samuel C. Gilman, a civil engineer, had come to the
Puget Sound country from St. Cloud, Minnesota, in February
1889, and during a journey to the Satsop River area, he "heard a
great deal about the unexplored Olympic Mountains." He returned
to Minnesota the following summer and told his father, Charles A.
Gilman, and his brother, John C. Gilman, what he had learned.

Although they had strong ties to Minnesota, where the father
had at one time served as lieutenant governor, the family decided
to move to the Pacific Northwest and then "traverse the
mountains and see what was really there." They arrived in
Centralia, Washington, in the fall of 1889. (The elder Gilman's
daughter and son-in-law lived in Grays Harbor City, having preceded the father and his sons.)

Charles and Samuel Gilman soon began exploring the Olympic Peninsula, doing so without fanfare and publicity, and—at
least on their first trek—without sponsor or benefactor. After
studying "the imperfect geography of the country," they concluded they could enter the Olympics more easily from the west
than from any other direction. Consequently, they traveled in a
boat down the Chehalis River to Grays Harbor. The water trip
began October 11 and lasted only two days, proving to be much
easier than a journey by stage.

The first trip the Gilmans made into the Olympic Mountains
began on October 17, 1889. The men purchased provisions in
Grays Harbor City, then traveled up the beach to Tahola, headquarters of the Quinault Indian Reservation, where they were
hospitably received by the agent. The autumn rains had been
falling steadily, and it was evident that winter was about to settle
over the mountains. Undaunted, the Gilmans sought a guide to
take them up the Quinault River, whose course they wished to

follow to its headwaters. The Indians, however, "shook their heads ominously, and muttered in their own peculiar, emotionless way something about the high water and deep snows, sure to be encountered." Because such an undertaking would be dangerous, "no prudent Indian was willing to expose himself to the terrors of snow and ice and water." Eventually, however, the Gilmans located an Indian who agreed to take them as far as the confluence of the North Fork and East Fork, about thirty or more airline miles northeast of the Indian Agency. (The distance they would actually travel, following the windings of the river, would approximate fifty miles.)

On October 20, "the two Gilmans, the Indian, and his klootchman [wife] and their baby," set out for Quinault Lake, poling the canoe upriver. The journey to the lake took two days. The Gilmans were impressed by the "surpassingly beautiful sheet of water . . . surrounded by steep, abrupt shores and almost impenetrable forests." The country had not, at that time, been settled by whites, but they did find three trappers living in a squatter's cabin that had been abandoned. The trappers were dubious when the Gilmans told them their plans, but the explorers were not discouraged, and continued up the river. "The

Charles Gilman (Photo courtesy Stearns County Historical Society Archives, St. Cloud, Minnesota)

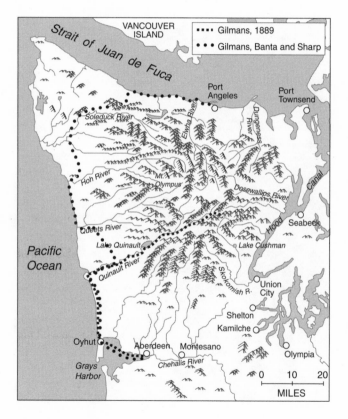

mountains, which had long been in the foreground, now rapidly closed in and swallowed them up." The Gilmans noted that foothills were practically nonexistent; the peaks to the east, their bases less than a mile distant, "at once lifted themselves boldly into the sky at heights of from 4,000 to 5,000 feet."

Because the river was now quite swift, the adventurers had to walk most of the time, the Indians pulling the canoe and ferrying them now and then across the river to take advantage of better traveling on the opposite side. Late in the afternoon of October 25, they reached the confluence of the river's two branches. This was the place where they had agreed the Indians would leave them, but the party remained together three days, while the guide proceeded up the East Fork and killed four elk, "which he salted down to take home with him."

On October 28, the Gilmans took the canoe and started up the East Fork, "which came down from the direction of Mount Constance." They had gone less than three miles, however, when they came to an immense log jam and were forced to abandon the canoe. The men then "shouldered their blankets, weapons, provisions and camping outfit and set out on foot," traveling overland up the valley.

Along the way, they climbed a peak which their aneroid barometer indicated was forty-three hundred feet high. On this mountain they first encountered snow. However, they remained overnight on the summit, and the weather, although chilly, was not severely cold. The men returned to the river, resumed their journey, and three days later were within two miles of the base of what they thought was Mount Constance—although it must have been Mount Anderson or another peak in that vicinity. Evidently, they were now in the heart of the mountains, near the head of what we know today as Enchanted Valley. They were shut in on every hand by fierce, overhanging peaks, "and they found their way, during sunless days, over difficult paths and trails strewn with a profusion of rocks and logs." The elk trails now became more numerous, and they followed them through the dense underbrush, "only to return to the water and to continue their difficult way." They could see that the sun was shining brightly far up the mountainsides, but its rays did not pierce the gloom of the valley, nor remove the moisture from overhanging boughs and underbrush, "upon which the frosts of the chilly nights hung in clots the livelong day." Both ground and air were damp, "and the water dripping from the trees added much to their discomfort." The mountains everywhere were "wildly rugged and broken, and it looked as if they would never dare climb their precipitous sides." The men noted that the slopes were marked, here and there, by long, deep trails, evidently the paths of great landslides that had torn down the mountainsides, in their "irresistible course down to the valley below." Often they saw

where many of the "great masses of rock and earth" had begun to slide. At times whole ledges, weakened by melting snow, had torn loose and dashed downward with overpowering momentum, leaving huge barren patches exposed. Sometimes the slide had begun so far up that they could not discern where it originated, the track disappearing in the heights.

The Gilmans decided to climb several peaks in order to view the country. After much travel, they reached several summits, "but the skies were so thick with fog that nothing could be seen." Their provisions were running low, but each man shot an elk and the kills provided enough meat to sustain them. They now saw numerous elk, but, having an ample supply of meat, did not molest the animals.

During their journey up the valley, the Gilmans had observed a lofty peak to the south, and they decided to climb it; however, the steep slopes made the ascent not only hazardous but also slow and laborious. Night overtook them shortly after they reached the snow line, so they camped in the snow, gathered brush for their fire, and cooked their supper. The slope was so steep that when they lay down to sleep they were forced to prop their feet against logs to keep from sliding down the mountain. The next day they toiled up through the snow to the summit, where "the view that burst upon their bewildered vision was glorious beyond description. The morning was clear and beautiful and their sight was limited only by the far-distant horizon."

Almost twenty miles northwest rose Mount Olympus, "covered with glittering snow," and they could see the last of a range of foothills strung out in descending succession to the west, and parallel with the Strait of Juan de Fuca. Mount Constance, "abrupt and lonely," stood ten miles to the northeast, "its lofty summit piercing the sky above all its immediate neighbors." The Cascades were visible far to the east, "with Mount Rainier rising grandly to the right and Mount Baker on the extreme left." Hood Canal, bordered with fir and cedar, looked like "a shining thread at their feet"; beyond it, Puget Sound was discernible. Seattle was lost in haze, but miles away, in the opposite direction, Grays Harbor and Quinault Lake could both be seen. The whole vista was so splendid it fixed itself indelibly upon the minds of "the two lonely beholders."

Their aneroid barometer indicated they were sixty-eight hundred feet above sea level, and the mountain was so positioned that they could not only see a great distance, but were also rewarded with "a commanding view of the hills and vales and water courses." Reluctant to leave, the men attempted to follow the crest but found themselves "impeded by insurmountable rocks and crevices." They descended the south slope, where the bluffs were so steep "they had to let themselves down with ropes." That night the Gilmans camped on the mountain,

then completed the descent the next day. On November 9 they reached a stream. Rain fell incessantly for four days, and the men suffered severely, especially at night, because their blankets were saturated. The trees and undergrowth were soaked, and one night it took them four hours to start a fire. When they eventually succeeded, "their gratitude knew no bounds."

When they reached the Quinault again, they were entirely without provisions, but they caught three salmon. They spent two nights in comparative comfort at this spot, but when they looked back upon the mountains they had just left, they saw that the peaks were now heavily burdened with snow. Had the men delayed their return one day, they could easily have perished.

The Gilmans then started down the river, keeping vigilant lookout for an old canoe they had noticed on their way up. They patched it, then resumed their journey down the East Fork, and upon arriving at its juncture with the North Fork, met two trappers. Here they recuperated for several days, resting and fishing. The rest of their trip was without incident—down the Quinault to the lake, then to the ocean, and southward on the beach to Grays Harbor City, where they arrived November 27, the day before Thanksgiving.

The Gilmans had entered the Olympic Mountains from the southwest, via the Quinault, but the record is not clear just how far they went or precisely where; apparently, however, they reached the divide between streams flowing east and west. The peaks they climbed were probably those clustered around Anderson Pass. They reconnoitered a large segment of the Olympics and acquainted themselves with its features. Obviously, they could have crossed the divide and descended the Dosewallips or the Duckabush to Hood Canal, but they appear to have had no desire to do so, and left the mountains by retracing their route in reverse.

The newspapers took little notice of their accomplishment, giving the journey cursory attention. Later Samuel Gilman wrote an article called "Olympic Country" that was published in the April 1896 issue of *National Geographic*, together with a topographic map of the Olympic Peninsula. The narrative was primarily a description of the terrain, not an account of the Gilmans' daily activities during the exploration.

The rainy season was well under way, the onset of winter just three weeks ahead, when the Gilmans decided to again go forth to "traverse the unknown land between the mountains and the ocean." Acting this time on behalf of the Northern Pacific Railway, they set out in early December for Port Angeles, to map out "a possible route for a railroad" from that town to Grays Harbor. When they arrived in the village, they announced their intention of going through the Quillayute country, but could find no one willing to accompany them.

The Gilmans trekked westward to the Pysht River, then crossed a low divide to the Soleduck River. The weather was foul—a mixture of rain and snow—and a wearisome, if not dangerous, journey lay before them. On December 9, while traversing the Soleduck valley, they obtained lodging at a way place operated by men named Crosby and Harriss. Meanwhile, John J. Banta and S. Price Sharp were also out looking over the country. Banta was twenty-six years old, and he had recently come to the Pacific Northwest from Illinois. He and Sharp left Tacoma on December 3, and after scouting Puget Sound and the San Juan Islands, they went to the Olympic Peninsula and were now "in search of a homestead west of Port Townsend." On December 10 they walked—most of the way through rain and snow—from Pysht Bay across the divide to the Crosby and Harriss way place, a distance of some twenty miles.

At the way place, Banta and Sharp met the Gilmans, who had preceded them by a day. Charles Gilman then made them a proposition. He told them he and his son were looking for a railroad route, and if Banta and Sharp would accompany them to Grays Harbor, he would pay their expenses. Because they were out examining the land anyway, the Tacoma men readily agreed. All four then discussed the journey and estimated that traveling by foot down the west side of the peninsula to Grays Harbor would take three weeks.

The district the quartet proposed to explore had been the subject of articles in *West Shore* magazine and a newspaper, the *Seattle Post-Intelligencer*. The stories declared that the area had

never been entered by white men, but that two prospectors had gone far enough to look over the outer ranges into the unknown region. The prospectors were reported to have seen a lake surrounded by mountains and valleys, with streams flowing into the lake from all directions. The lake was believed to have a subterranean outlet to the sea. The reports also indicated that this paradise was inhabited by fierce cannibals, and therefore the other Indians were afraid to go there. In fact, it was claimed, anyone who dared to venture into the region faced almost certain death. Banta wrote in his diary that they did not believe these stories, nor did his party feel they would be in any danger, although they might get hungry at times due to a scarcity of provisions.

The men fashioned pack straps from heavy canvas, then started out on December 11, each man carrying sixty pounds. After traveling eight miles they put up that night with a settler. The land traversed during the day had been comparatively level, and bore the finest fir timber that Banta had ever seen. Although the streams were bordered by good bottomland, he felt the country was most valuable for the timber. He observed that settlement was ahead of the government survey, and the land was being "taken up very fast."

The Enchanted Valley was explored by the Gilmans (Photo by Frank O. Shaw)

The party reached the Forks post office on December 12. This establishment served a settlement on a prairie that lay between the Bogachiel and Soleduck rivers. The prairie land was all taken up, and much of it had been improved. Peter Fisher, a settler who had lived there for twelve years, had a good farm with a splendid orchard. He said that all kinds of fruit did well on the prairie. The community was thriving and boasted a water-powered sawmill.

Fisher told the men he had been "nearly all over this country," and said he had followed the rivers to their sources, looking for minerals, but had not been successful. The explorers employed the women at Fisher's place to make them a tent by splicing "wagon sheets." They also purchased pans, spoons, knives, and forks, as well as a supply of bacon, butter, coffee, and flour.

The men left Forks on December 13, each man carrying sixty pounds. Fisher accompanied them to the Bogachiel River, one and a half miles distant, and ferried them across in his canoe. The men then walked another mile and a half "and camped in the woods."

Because their packs were heavy, they usually traveled only four or five miles a day, pitching their tent somewhere in the forest. After crossing foothills, they reached the Hoh River two miles above its mouth, on December 17. The river was large and rapid, and when in flood had scattered huge piles of driftwood on the bottoms. Trees six feet in diameter and a hundred feet long had been stacked up like "sticks of kindling wood." The men thought the Hoh was the longest river they had crossed and believed it had its source "way up on the north side of Mt. Olympus." The next day they paid some Indians two dollars to take them by canoe to the ocean. Had they known "it was so short a distance," they "could have walked it easy."

About fifty Indians lived near the river's mouth. Most were barefoot, and one old man wore nothing but a calico shirt, but a few were well-dressed. The Indians thought the whites were "quite a curious looking set of men." Because some of them had attended the school on the Quinault reservation, the men were able to converse with them a little.

The explorers paid an Indian named Charley Misp three dollars to accompany them down the beach to the Queets River, to show the way and to keep them from getting caught by the tide. When they came to a large stream, Misp stripped and carried everyone across. "I think he made six trips across," Banta wrote in his diary, "before he got us and our baggage all across." He added that the men did not expect him to do this, "but made no kick about it."

When the men came down to the beach that afternoon, they had to climb the bank and wait four hours until the tide receded. They camped that night opposite Destruction Island, upon which they saw "quite a number of houses." The next morning they had to wait until midday for the tide to go out, then headed for the Queets. Misp told them he lived about a mile upstream, and invited them to remain overnight at his place, assuring them he had plenty of flour, salt salmon, coffee, and potatoes. He also had a boat in which they could travel up the river. This pleased the men because by now they were wet, cold, and much fatigued.

Darkness overtook the party by the time it reached the boat, but Misp told them they would soon arrive at his house. However, after the men sat quietly in the boat for an hour, getting "awful cold," they asked Misp how near to his house they were. He replied: "Half mile." After they had traveled that distance, they inquired again and received the same answer.

Banta speculated that if anyone had been near and had heard their teeth rattling, "they would have thought there was a hundred frogs hollering." Eventually, after going two miles up the river—and at one point almost capsizing—they pulled to shore, and the men followed their guide up a narrow path to his cabin. The house was seventy by thirty feet, and within it three fires were burning, with a different family crouched by each fire. An old woman sat alone in one corner with a little fire of her own. No one paid attention to her, nor she to them. "I suppose," Banta

wrote, "she had served her day and was of no use any longer, and was just waiting for the last fires of life to burn out."

The Indians were pleased by the men's visit, and Misp's wife prepared baking powder bread, boiled potatoes, salt salmon, and tea. When the meal was ready she spread a piece of canvas on a large platform (which they used for all purposes) and set before each man a plate, cup and saucer, knife and fork. Banta thought the table looked "quite tempting" to men who were as hungry as they, and he was sure they did it justice.

Misp had agreed to take the men up the Queets the next day, going as far as he could in two days. When morning came, the men remained in bed "untill real late," waiting for their host to rise, but he proved to be "a better stayer" than they. After a late breakfast, when they were ready to depart, Misp informed them he could not go that day. Because it was late, and he said he could leave the following morning, they "concluded to stop at the Misp house one day and night longer." They spent most of the day indoors because rain fell steadily.

Banta took advantage of the opportunity, during his intimate visit with the Indians, to observe their habits and customs. He

Mount LaCrosse, which may have been climbed by the Gilmans
(Photo by Frank O. Shaw)

noticed, for example, that when Mrs. Misp prepared supper, that she had a gut stuffed with elk tallow—"just like we put up sausage"—and that she rubbed the bread pan with it to keep the bread from sticking. She greased the pan well, then handed the gut to another woman, who rubbed it all over her face, and then her hair. After this woman had herself "well slicked up, another took it and went through the same performance." Banta then recorded another observation in his notebook: "Again I saw a bright little girl about eight years old go up to a bucket that had some water in it where we had all been drinking, and where there was a tin cup seting [sic] on either side of the bucket, but instead of using the tins, she just stuck her wooly head down into the bucket and supped the water from the bottom of the bucket."

On Sunday, December 22, the men hired two other Indians to take them ten miles up the Queets. Banta gained the mistaken impression that the river did not have its source high in the mountains, but gathered its waters among the foothills. Consequently, it was less swift, he thought, than the Hoh or the Quinault. The bottomland was level, of rich soil, averaging a mile in width.

They camped that night six miles up the river on a gravel bar. The next day, Banta discovered the place where he wanted to homestead—on the northwest side, eight miles upriver from the ocean.

The men broke camp early on December 24, and left the Queets as they headed toward the Quinault, traveling through heavy stands of cedar and thick brush. They spent Christmas Eve camped on a ridge. Banta observed they had plenty of places to hang their socks, "but not much prospect of getting them filled with presents."

Christmas Day dawned clear, but not very cold, with about two inches of snow on the ground. The men saw a band of about a dozen elk, but didn't get a shot at them in time to replenish their larder. Early that afternoon they came to a large stream, which they took to be the Raft River, or possibly a tributary of the Queets. They had a good view of the country to the north and west, and they judged the distance from the ocean to the foothills to be about twenty-five miles.

During the next few days, the men found travel to be difficult because it involved clambering over a succession of ridges, as well as floundering through cedar swamps. The snow depth remained the same, and rain fell much of the time. As a result, the bushes were "wet with snow and water," and the men's clothing was soaked. Their provisions were almost gone, and Banta commented rather pointedly in his diary: "I would rather be in Tacoma." By December 27, they were traveling on half rations.

The men reached the Quinault River on December 28, striking it about twenty miles from the ocean. They now had just enough flour for half a meal the next morning, plus a small slice of bacon each. But they had plenty of coffee and tea. Their situation was not desperate, but the men were beginning to suspect they might get pretty hungry before they got anything to eat, since the nearest Indians lived about fifteen miles down the river. The explorers had planned to travel cross-country to the Humptulips, but realizing this was now impossible, they decided to build a makeshift canoe in which to float down the river.

Utilizing a log two feet in diameter and twenty-six feet long, they began construction of the crude craft on Sunday, December 29. They were digging out the log—a slow, tedious job—when they noticed ducks flying downstream, and they surmised that someone was coming down the river. They quit working and shortly afterward four men came by in a boat. They had been staking claims above Quinault Lake, and they, too, had run out of provisions and hence could not spare anything, nor could they take everyone down the river in their boat. Charles Gilman volunteered to go with them to the nearest Indian home and hire the Indians to come up the next day and get the men, and also bring them something to eat.

The men did not resume work on the canoe because they felt

John J. Banta and family members (Photo courtesy Grace Lapham and Lelia Barney)

they could hold out better if they didn't labor. All they did was keep up a good fire, a necessity because the weather was stormy. They ate their last bread that night, but saved the bacon for breakfast. When it was just about dark, Sam Gilman shot a grouse that lit in a nearby tree, and this made them feel that they could have a good dinner and sleep late the next morning. They had a little flour left, and with it made "some nice grouse soup."

On Monday, December 30, their bill of fare for breakfast consisted of three full cups of grouse soup to each man, and plenty of coffee. Banta and Sharp then climbed a burned hill, from where they had an excellent view. "We got back to camp wet and cold and hungry," Banta wrote. "We had nothing to do but keep up the fire, and go hungry untill the Indians came, let it be one day or a week."

About five o'clock they heard the Indians shooting a gun. They soon came into sight, landed, and gave the men the "grub" that Gilman had sent—potatoes, flour, salt salmon, and three loaves of bread. The bread disappeared rapidly, long before supper was ready. The Indians had made a quick trip. Gilman had not reached their house until ten o'clock that morning, having stood all night around a campfire in the storm because he had no tent. He told the Indians that the men were out of food and that, if they did not reach them that night, he would not pay in full the seven dollars that he had promised them if they transported the men to the Indian Agency at the mouth of the river.

On the last day of December, the Indians and whites traveled down the Quinault about fifteen miles to the Indians' home. While the Indians ate their dinner, the explorers warmed themselves by the fire. They arrived at the Agency in mid-afternoon. Among the whites here were the agent, the government teamster, and the reservation physician. The white men insisted that the explorers take supper with them, sleep in the store room, and have breakfast with them the next morning. The evening was devoted to conversation, and the explorers learned much about the customs and habits of the Indians. Eventually, the talk languished, and they bid the old year goodbye and rolled themselves in their blankets.

On New Year's Day, 1890, the men breakfasted with the agent, then hired an Indian to haul them and their baggage to Oyhut, the landing place on Grays Harbor, about twenty-five miles distant. The beach served as the road. The day was cold and windy, with snowflakes flying through the air. Each man wrapped himself in a double blanket, but in order to keep warm they had to walk half the time.

They arrived at Oyhut that evening. The government teamster had loaned them the key to his house, and they were glad to get out of the storm. The cabin contained food, stoves, and beds. Snow fell during the night, and the weather was foul the next morning, snow falling and the wind blowing fiercely. The man who ran the sailboat from Oyhut to Grays Harbor City was away, but the tideflats were freezing and he would not be able to land should he return. The men were "pretty well boxed up," but there was enough food in the house, so they could stay as long as they wished.

On January 4, in subzero weather, the men took the sailboat to Grays Harbor City. At this point the Gilmans parted company with Banta and Sharp. The latter checked into a hotel, while the Gilmans proceeded to the home of Charles Gilman's son-in-law.

The end result of this "daring trip through the Olympic Peninsula in winter" was unexpected. The Gilmans had been looking for a railroad route on the west side of the peninsula between Port Angeles and Grays Harbor, but no railroad was ever built. The result was that the overland journey "led to the colonization of the Queets and Clearwater valleys." This was effected by Banta and Sharp. Upon their return to Tacoma, they began "making arrangements to organize a colony" on the Queets, and twenty-one claims were taken that spring. The men worked hard to promote the project, which eventually became known as "Evergreen on the Queets." Banta made six trips to the Queets in 1890 with prospective homesteaders. The following spring the men chartered a steamship and transported settlers to the Queets on two occasions. The colony flourished during the half-century from 1890 until 1940, when the land was added to Olympic National Park.

After they explored the Olympic Peninsula, the Gilmans returned to Minnesota.

Samuel Charles Gilman was the eldest of fourteen children. He died suddenly from blood poisoning in 1896, in St. Cloud, Minnesota. He was thirty-six years old.

Charles Andrew Gilman, the father of Samuel, outlived eight of his fourteen children (seven sons and seven daughters). He died in St. Cloud in 1927, age ninety-four. A long-time resident of St. Cloud and Sauk Rapids, he had a distinguished political career that spanned more than half a century. He served in nine state legislatures, was elected speaker of the house for three terms, and also served as lieutenant governor for three terms.

4

Across the Olympic Mountains

EUGENE SEMPLE, GOVERNOR OF WASH-ington Territory, wrote eloquently about the unknown Olympics in his 1888 report to the Department of the Interior. The next year, Elisha P. Ferry, governor-elect of Washington State, told a reporter from the *Seattle Press* of the need to explore the Olympic Mountains. Ferry indulged in a bit of hyperbole. Washington, he declared, had her great unknown land "like the interior of Africa": the opportunity was present for someone to acquire fame by unveiling the mystery encircled by the snow-capped peaks.

As a result of the governor's interview, the *Seattle Press* received numerous inquiries, with several men stating they planned to explore the Olympics during the summer of 1890. Perhaps they knew little of what such an endeavor demanded, but one letter aroused unusual interest. Dated November 6, 1889, it was written by James H. Christie, who said he was prepared to enter the Olympics at once, not wait until summer. This sounded rash, but Christie had lived in northern lands "beyond the limits of civilization." Because he was short of funds, Christie suggested the newspaper outfit an expedition.

Accompanied by John H. Crumback, Christopher Hayes, and John W. Sims, Christie arrived in Seattle in late November to confer with William E. Bailey, the newspaper's proprietor. Bailey was sufficiently impressed by the men that he decided to sponsor the expedition. Charles A. Barnes and Dr. Harris B. Runnalls were then added to the party, but before the expedition lost contact with civilization the doctor had to withdraw, leaving the party limited to five men. They were described as having an "abundance of grit and manly vim." They would need it because they had chosen to tackle an unknown wilderness at the onset of winter—a winter that they had no reason to suspect would be one of the severest ever recorded in the Pacific Northwest.

According to the *Press*, the expedition planned to gather scientific information, describe the topography, note the presence or absence of minerals, estimate the quality and quantity of the timber, and determine whether or not colonization was practical. The explorers were not to rush through the Olympics, but would start in the winter "in order to be over the first ranges and into the central valleys ready for work when spring should open." This, however, was camouflage to mask the true reason the expedition was hastily organized—the likelihood that whoever received the honor of crossing the Olympics first would have to do so that winter, because interest in exploring the region had flared to a high pitch as a result of the governor's clarion call.

The *Press* outfitted the men with a ton of provisions and equipment—everything thought necessary to make a complete exploration. The explorers planned to subsist primarily upon game, but ample quantities of flour, bacon, beans, coffee, and other staples were provided. The equipment included rifles, ammunition, a tent, canvas sheets, blankets, rubber boots, oilskin, fishing tackle, axes, snowshoes, cooking utensils, and various tools. They also had enough film to make a photographic record of the country traversed. Lastly, they were given fifty pounds of "colored fire" (fireworks) with which to illuminate, on a specified date, a peak visible from Seattle.

The expedition, complete with three dogs, left the city in early December and traveled to Port Angeles, where the men called upon the town's "leading citizens" to get information. However,

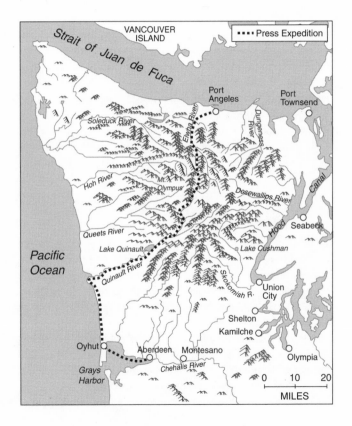

they learned little about what lay beyond the foothills and first ranges. Relying upon the advice he received, Christie decided to build a flatboat with which to transport everything up the Elwha River. But first they had to get to the river, so they moved their headquarters to a ranch five miles west of Port Angeles.

A rough, winding trail led from the ranch toward the river, but it was in deplorable condition. Beyond its terminus a way had to be cut through dense undergrowth and fallen timber. When this work had been accomplished, the men packed their equipage and supplies to the banks of the Elwha. Meanwhile, Barnes, the deputy leader, obtained two pack mules from a settler, and Christie arranged to have the lumber for the boat hauled from a sawmill.

The expedition made its first camp on December 19 at a point overlooking the river. By the evening of December 23, the entire outfit had been packed to this site. That night snow began falling heavily, and trees fell all around the camp, keeping everyone awake. By daylight the snow was a foot deep. The men "kept a monster fire going day and night," as the snow continued to fall, but Christmas Day broke clear and cold, with everything frozen stiff. Undaunted, the men cleared the path and packed lumber to the building site, and that evening they did ample justice to their Christmas dinner of bacon and beans.

Unable to use the mules at this time, the men took them to

The Press Expedition, photographed in Seattle, December 6, 1889. Left to right, *Sims, Runnalls, Barnes, Christie, Crumback, and Hayes.* (Photo courtesy Mrs. Pierre Barnes)

the claim of William D. Macdonald, four miles upriver, "to be left until called for." Building their boat was difficult because the green lumber was sodden with water, frozen stiff, and covered with ice. The men kept a huge fire going to thaw the wood, which they caulked as well as they could, but they were doubtful of the results. They finished the construction in four days, and prepared to launch the boat on December 31. Snow still fell incessantly, but the men struck camp and packed the supplies to the launching site, then slid the boat into the water—christening her *Gertie* as they did so. The boat swept out into the deep water, and the men stretched the towline and pulled her through the rapids—she was light, without cargo.

"No burst of music or libations of wine" celebrated the occasion, but the men considered the launch to be a huge success. While a roaring campfire battled falling snow, the explorers feasted on pea soup, boiled ham, baked beans, corn bread, and prune pie—all washed down with "deep potations of Java best." The men then loaded *Gertie* with cargo, but when her upper seams went below the surface, "she began to take in water like a thirsty fish."

The outlook for the Press Expedition now looked gloomy. The exploration had been under way almost a month, but the men were still on the lower Elwha. They would have to recaulk and relaunch the boat before they could proceed. Because snow fell heavily again on New Year's Day, Christie became somewhat concerned. When the men awoke the next morning, snow was still falling and their camp was deeply buried. Work on the trail was impossible, and by the morning of January 3, the snow was three and a half feet deep, with much deeper drifts in places.

Nevertheless, the men hauled the boat out, then dried and recaulked her. The weather remained "devilish cold." They prepared a landing place, turned the boat over, built fires beneath her, and spread awning overhead. For a week the boat was kept hot both day and night, and when relaunched on January 12, she "floated like a duck."

The expedition was now able to start its long-delayed trip up the Elwha, but handling the boat was difficult because the river wound around bluffs, with deep water on first one side, then the other. The strong current at times churned the water to foam, then ran deep and swift, "like a mill race." The towrope had to be manned from first one side, then the other, wherever footholds could be secured. This often caused the men to be in water above their boot tops, occasionally to their waists. The temperature was about fifteen degrees below freezing, and whenever a man stepped out of the water his clothing froze almost instantly.

A large logjam created a dam across the Elwha at the mouth of Indian Creek. The local settlers used this obstruction as a bridge because they had no other way to cross. The Indians and settlers who lived nearby helped the explorers portage *Gertie* over this barrier, and when the maneuver had been accomplished, they were "one more step towards Olympus."

The pattern of events for a number of days was steady snowfall, and men spending much time in icy water as they slowly progressed southward. When they approached Macdonald's ranch, where they had taken the mules, the men were unable to pull the loaded boat due to the low state of the river, and for the first time Christie expressed doubt that this method of transport was feasible. "I am afraid that I will be compelled to give up the boat and take to the trail," he wrote, "as the depth of snow on the bank, through which the boys must plow their way makes progress devilish slow, tedious and disagreeable." Shortly afterward, he decided to abandon *Gertie* as soon as they brought up the balance of the stores.

The men had had enough of *Gertie*, after struggling with the craft for almost two weeks, during which time they had moved the expedition's camp only four miles. On Friday, January 24, they stripped the boat and stored her in a comfortable berth.

Christie had no intention of abandoning the exploration, since the equipment and provisions could be transported by other means. If the snow melted they would use the mules; if the snow froze and formed a hard crust, they could fashion "land vehicles" such as sledges and travois; finally, if the snow remained soft, the men would wear snowshoes and backpack the supplies. But the snow did none of these things; it continued to fall, and had now reached a depth of five feet, confining the explorers to Macdonald's cabin. With the approach of February, the Press Expedition had been under way nearly two months, but the men were still low in the Elwha valley, not yet past the last squatter's cabin. Although they did not realize it, the various delays had served them well, keeping them out of the heart of the Olympics during the dead of winter.

With unbounded optimism, the men now built various contrivances with which to transport their loads. No two vehicles were alike, and none worked. The long-awaited heavy frost occurred, but the thin crust that formed during the night became slush shortly after the sun rose. When the vehicles were weighted with cargo, their runners sank to the deck. Unless they were to abandon the exploration, the men would have to backpack everything.

Each man shouldered fifty pounds. Their snowshoes sank six to eight inches in the soft snow, making backpacking fatiguing, but by the first day's end they had packed eight hundred pounds for a mile and a half over a rough, steep trail. This was the first of many days of backpacking.

Because the expedition had a ton of stores and equipage, the material had to be carried in successive stages. With each man packing fifty pounds, they could transport two hundred fifty pounds per trip. Therefore, at least eight trips were required to transport everything from one campsite to the next; stated differently, in order to move the expedition one mile, they had to walk fifteen miles (carrying heavy loads for eight miles, going back unloaded for seven).

Christie now began sending out reconnaissance parties before moving the expedition to new camps. On February 10, the men saw "the cabin of . . . another absentee squatter," the second one they had come to that was beyond the supposed "limit of settlement." Next, they followed an old trail to the foot of a bluff known as the Devil's Backbone. The path then climbed high, traversing the bluff's face, and Christie noted it would have to be improved before the supplies could be packed over it, which was done.

Once everything was transported over the bluff, the expedition finally reached "The Forks," the *ultima thule* of exploration by the local settlers. During breakfast at this camp, the men spied two wolves across the river. Sims shot one, then killed a bobcat, and the men named two nearby streams Wolf Creek and Cat Creek.

James H. Christie after he returned from exploring the Canadian Northwest, 1886–88 (Photo courtesy Robert B. Hitchman)

With the arrival of March, the snow remained deep and soft, making travel difficult. Nevertheless, Barnes left The Forks to search for a route ahead. He traveled up the west side of the Elwha through a canyon. Because the terrain was rough, he did not reach the canyon's head until the third morning, when he caught sight of a lovely valley below. He followed a ravine and then beheld a scene that caused him to pause in wonder. Along one side of the little valley, the river, bounded by a sheer rock wall, thundered in great rapids; then the stream appeared to come to a standstill in a deep, green pool, where it swirled around and formed a giant eddy, abruptly made a right angle turn, and glided through a narrow cleft in the cliff and disappeared in the distance. When he looked down the canyon, Barnes saw "a multitude of faces" at the water's edge. The explorers later named the place Goblin Gates. Because the bottomland ahead looked promising, Barnes waded the river and returned to camp on the east side.

Christie now felt he could use the mules, but the men had to travel downriver to retrieve them. Unfortunately, during the return trip one of the mules lost its footing as they traversed the formation called the Devil's Backbone, and was fatally injured. The animal's load had consisted of one hundred fifty pounds of

Charles Adams Barnes, deputy leader of the Press Expedition
(Photo courtesy Mrs. Pierre Barnes)

flour and fifty pounds of "colored fire." By now the men had become practical explorers. They retrieved the flour, but kicked the "hell fire" down the mountainside. They arrived at the expedition's camp at dark—cold, wet, and discouraged. The lost mule had been the heavier of the two pack animals, and they had depended on her to transport the bulk of their supplies. Now they would have to do the work themselves.

Backpacking was tedious and tiring, and the rigors of the journey were beginning to affect the men's health. All became ill with dysentery. On March 16, Christie and Crumback reconnoitered upriver to gain information about the country ahead. Upon reaching a point that overlooked the terrain, they observed, in Christie's words, "a grand chain of peaks as far as the eye could reach, an exquisite panorama of mountain scenery to a lover of solitary natural grandeur." Enraptured with the scene before him, Christie turned to Crumback and demanded if he did not think it glorious. He was shocked to hear his companion reply, in low but impressive tones, that he considered it a "damned rough layout."

Now the weather had turned warm, rain showers were frequent, and the melting snow was soft. The expedition was within the winter range of deer and, since the animals were numerous, the explorers called this Deer Range. Because they were exhausted from days of backpacking heavy loads, the men were glad to see a valley where they could recuperate and strengthen themselves for ordeals yet ahead. On March 20, they dropped down to the river bottom and set up camp near the Elwha. The expedition spent almost two weeks in this little paradise because the men needed to rest, repair clothes, reconnoiter the adjacent territory, and make pemmican to add to their stores. Their surviving mule was also permitted to rest for a week.

The little "oasis in the desert of snow" won everyone's affection, so much so that Crumback decided to settle there after the expedition ended. This was unsurveyed public domain which could be held only by "squatting" on the claim until the land had been surveyed. Undaunted, Crumback decided to build the foundation of his cabin, and the other men agreed to assist. On the opening day of spring, 1890, they set to work, and within fifteen minutes had the foundation in place. They declared this to be the first cabin in the Olympic Mountains—which was hardly the truth—and blazed a nearby fir, inscribing upon it the words: "John Crumback, his claim." The men then returned to camp to celebrate. Crumback acted as host and prepared a royal banquet. The menu consisted of elk tail broth, fresh trout, and roast venison, plus an extra allowance of bread with their coffee.

This easy life contrasted sharply with the one they had endured in the winter months. Because deer were plentiful, the men now lived chiefly upon fresh meat. They kept themselves busy repairing articles, caching unnecessary items, going on reconnaissance, hunting, drying fish, and preparing pemmican. During the evening hours they fished for salmon and trout.

While encamped in the valley, the men heard strange, whirring noises which they attributed, at first, to avalanches. Eventually, they concluded the sounds might come from a geyser. They were unable to take the time to search for it, and left the task to future explorers, but they did name the place Geyser Valley. (The "future explorers" had no better luck. Thirty years later visitors heard motorboats instead of geysers. Nothing has ever been found to explain the noises heard by the Press party, but the general belief today is that the men were deceived by the elusive drumming of grouse.)

The Press Expedition had now been under way for almost four months, but it had not yet penetrated the mountains to a great depth. In fact, the men had barely gotten beyond the foothills with which the settlers were familiar. As the raven flies, the expedition was now located about a dozen miles south of the camp where the upriver trek began. The explorers had, however, blazed a crude trail as they slowly moved up the Elwha. They had been faced constantly with the problem of route finding. They had done much hard work: building *Gertie*, pulling her upriver, clearing and blazing the way, and relaying supplies and equipment from camp to camp. Now the expedition had to move much faster

if the men were to succeed in crossing the mountains. The *Press* had stated that the party would explore the country thoroughly and not rush through. The expedition had been provisioned for six months, and two-thirds of that time had gone by. If they were to succeed in going across the Olympics—and this was beginning to look doubtful—they must still travel four times as far as they had come. Ahead were the highest, most rugged peaks, where more adventures and hardships awaited, and where they still had to find a route to the Quinault River. The Olympics were just beginning to test their "abundance of grit and manly vim."

During one scouting trip, the men had glimpsed a valley some miles ahead that was far larger than Geyser Valley, "and from which four passes or gaps appeared to radiate like the spokes of a wagon wheel." Believing it would serve admirably as a base camp, Christie made it their next objective. He decided to cache their provisions on the Lillian River—a tributary of the Elwha just beyond Geyser Valley—and reconnoiter, before bringing up the supplies. They would travel light and live off the land, therefore everything not needed was securely cached. The men then headed up the Elwha, with one hundred pounds on the mule and the men carrying the camp outfit. As they proceeded, the country became rougher, the snow deeper, and logs, snow, and forest debris often lay so thick that they had a difficult time in forcing a passage. Eventually, they found a level place to camp that night, but the snow was waist deep, and the mule had nothing to eat. They gave her a few of their precious beans, but she obtained "most of her provender" by chewing the indigestible fir boughs the men cut for their bed. That night the party was battered by torrential rains.

The men were concerned, and with good reason. The mountains were not opening out into a big central valley, as the legends promised. Instead, the country was becoming increasingly rugged, the mountainsides steeper, the snow deeper. Now, for the first time, the explorers began to wonder whether they had provisions enough to enable them to cross the Olympics. Game was scarce because they had left the winter range of elk and deer. Below the Lillian River they had lived mainly on fresh meat and fish, and they had expected that beyond the Lillian they would find game as easily as before. Consequently, they had brought no meat with them on the scouting trip. They went hunting but were unsuccessful, and could do nothing but return to the cache on the Lillian. When they started back they had had nothing to eat for breakfast except tea and unleavened flour cakes, but during the return trip they luckily found and killed two elk.

The men spent the next week relaying provisions to the lower

John W. Sims in British Army uniform (Photo courtesy Sims's daughter Mary Buell)

"Side of Mountain, May 1st," Press Expedition photograph (Photo courtesy Robert B. Hitchman)

end of Press Valley, the name they had given to their next objective. After they had set up camp, Christie and Barnes climbed the slope behind the camp to make observations, and were surprised to come upon a sort of level plateau about one and a half miles long, by a third as wide, which they mistakenly took—upon finding a circular mound which did not appear to be natural—to be the site of an old Indian village. Because it reminded them of the legends related by Governor Eugene Semple, they named it Semple Plateau. Above the plateau they followed an elk trail until they came to a jutting rock which they named The Gallery, for the splendid views and the photographs they obtained there.

Finally, the Press Expedition had penetrated deep into the mountains, and whenever the men climbed high enough to observe the country, they saw rugged, snowy peaks in all directions. They found the topography confusing, but they had to decide whether to continue following the Elwha or look elsewhere for a route across. To solve the problem, a scouting party set out on April 19 to search for a good route to the southwest. If a pass existed, and they chose to use it, the expedition would be diverted from the Elwha, the river they had followed from the beginning of their journey. They could, of course, continue to follow the Elwha, but would it lead them to the Quinault?

Late that afternoon the men reached a viewpoint and saw what appeared to be a pass to the southwest, and they decided that they should angle westward. This was a momentous decision, one upon which they would reflect later. The westward gap seemed to be a logical route, and beyond it they could see a snowy range that appeared to be the backbone of the mountains. They named it Bailey Range, after their publisher sponsor, then returned to camp.

The men began moving the expedition's camp from Press Valley to Semple Plateau, then ascended the slope that led to The Gallery and beyond, constantly on the lookout for a campsite where water was available. Near The Gallery tragedy struck twice in rapid succession. One of their dogs was killed by a bull elk; then their exhausted mule collapsed, and all of their endeavors—including striking her with a club—could not induce her to rise. They unloaded her, cached the pack she had been carrying, and turned her loose to forage for herself.

Men and dogs went on, and that night they camped in the dark beside a snow-covered creek. Taking stock of their grim situation, they calculated that, by traveling as lightly and rapidly as possible, they could not reach Quinault Lake in less than a month, and it might take two. They still had one hundred fifty pounds of flour, twenty-five pounds of beans, ten pounds of bacon, five pounds of salt, and less than two pounds of tobacco. They also had sixty pounds of smoked meat. On a full rations

"On the Divide" [Low Divide], Press Expedition photograph
(Photo courtesy Robert B. Hitchman)

basis, these provisions would not last more than ten days, but the men felt they "could be made to last indefinitely" if they rationed themselves severely.

Heading west, the men followed the gloomy canyon of an Elwha tributary, which they named the Goldie River in honor of a friend. The men had now left the Elwha and had irrevocably set their course to the southwest, believing it would lead them to the Quinault. Unwittingly, they had chosen to cross one of the most rugged parts of the Olympics, an area that is without man-made trails to this day. They slept on the snow because bare ground was nowhere to be found. No longer could they take the time to rest in camp or go hunting. Each day they plodded slowly forward on snowshoes, and they became increasingly aware of the necessity to reduce their packs to the lightest possible weight. They therefore discarded many items, and they retained only the clothes they wore. They had begun the trip with very good clothing, but they were now in rags and looked like tramps. Their boots were falling apart; their hats they had long since cast aside.

Bidding the Goldie River good-bye, they climbed straight up the mountainside, each man carrying a sixty-pound pack. The slope was steep, covered with snow ten to fifteen feet deep, and they had to kick footholds, sometimes sinking five or six feet at each step. Undaunted, they climbed with the hope that they would be across the main divide three days later. One night, however, disaster struck again. Their starving dogs stole most of their remaining bacon. The one piece they had left contained very little fat—the only "grease" they had. Except for a meager allowance, the men had been without much fat for nearly two months, and this dietary lack was beginning to affect their health.

The explorers were now in the "high country," where

everything except the trees was covered with snow, making it pointless to look for a bare campsite. While the other men went back to bring up the second load, Christie and Barnes climbed "above the timber belt" to a point where they could "see over the divide ahead." This was an important moment because they could now, for the first time, see the Quinault watershed. However, they were almost stunned by the "sea of mountains" lying across the path leading to their journey's end. Using the utmost economy they would have enough food for only twelve days. However, they *could* see the Quinault, the object of all their travel, separated from them at a distance of perhaps six or seven miles by a divide somewhat lower than the height at which they were now standing. But what a route.

Christie and Barnes decided it was a case of "one pack [to] a man." No longer would they relay supplies from one camp to the next; no more would they go back to a former camp to bring up additional provisions. They would simply strike out and keep going. Both men felt relieved by this decision. By taking with them only what they could pack in a single load, and traveling steadily, they could expect to reach Quinault Lake and game country in ten or twelve days. They could make it sooner if the way turned out to be better than it appeared; "worse than it appeared, it could not be." All they could take would be their dwindling stock of food, the guns and ammunition, the camera

and a few instruments, and half a blanket each. Once they neared the lake, the men had no doubt that they could obtain game and fish, but their experience of the last twenty-five miles forbade them to expect game any sooner than that. Christie and Barnes spent the next hour photographing and taking the bearings of peaks, the courses of streams and canyons. They also named several mountains.

The next day, the explorers prepared for the journey ahead. They divided the gear to be taken into five packs and cached the remainder. All day, while they worked, they heard the roar of avalanches. The heavy snows burdening the peaks had become unstable due to the warm spring weather, and the men realized they would have to use extreme caution when traversing the steep slopes.

The expedition had taken almost five months to reach the midpoint between its starting place, on the Elwha, and Quinault Lake, where the men hoped to leave the mountains. They still had to travel as far as they had gone from early December to the end of April. However, they were now on the central divide (or so they thought), and once they crossed it their path would lead downhill. Nevertheless, the route was an unknown one, a way that still held surprises.

They broke camp at daylight on May 1. Despite months of hardship, the men's morale was high, and the magic phrase

"homeward bound!" was constantly in their thoughts. Each man's pack weighed about seventy-five pounds. After trudging upward for two and one-half hours, they attained the point where Christie and Barnes had made observations the day before. All that day they traversed steep slopes bare of timber and heavy with blinding snow, and they were in constant fear of avalanches. Late in the afternoon they came to a huge rock, bare on its outward face, sticking out of the snow. When they looked over the edge, they saw warm, dry shelves below. They decided to camp here, each man selecting his berth and making himself as secure as possible. The view was magnificent, but the perches were neither comfortable nor safe. No one slept much because they were afraid they would fall off the mountain.

The next day proved to be even more strenuous because the terrain was broken by ravines. Upon reaching what they took to be the divide, the men believed they would now have a downhill route the rest of the way. They were standing upon a narrow ridge, obviously atop a watershed, but something was wrong. Far below, a valley and stream stretched across their line of travel. Realizing this was not the Quinault, the men speculated as to its identity,

The Press Expedition, photographed in Aberdeen, Washington, May 21, 1890. Left to right, *Sims, Barnes, Crumback (kneeling), Christie, and Hayes.* (Photo courtesy Mrs. Pierre Barnes and Mary Buell)

and the fear crept into their minds that it might be the Elwha. This was shortly confirmed. Upon leaving the Elwha to follow the Goldie, the men had cut a base line across a vast curve of the former, and in so doing had traveled over twenty miles of the roughest terrain, only to find themselves on the divide between the Elwha and the Goldie. Had they stayed with the Elwha, they could have made the journey on snowshoes in two days. Such is the fate of explorers. They were somewhat consoled by the fact that the gap they had taken to be the Quinault still looked like the Quinault. All they could do was descend to the Elwha, then climb the opposite side. They started down, and four hours later stood upon the valley floor. The men selected a place by the Elwha, shoveled it clear, and made camp. Because they were "completely tuckered out," they rested the next day. Their food had, for several days, consisted solely of "flour soup"—a mixture of flour, salt, and boiling water. This proved to be filling—and, when coupled with hunger, tasted quite good.

On May 4, the men broke camp and headed up the valley toward the gap between the peaks they had named Mount Seattle and Mount Christie. They faced a steep climb to the divide. But first they crossed the Elwha, then removed their moccasins and snowshoes and put on their boots in order to kick steps as they climbed. Higher up, the way was barred for six hundred feet by bare rock ledges. Up these they climbed, utilizing their rope for a lifeline. When they reached the top, they

John W. Sims with his daughter Mary, about 1913 (Photo courtesy Mary Buell)

were exhausted—"more from the expenditure of nervous force than by physical." By sundown, however, they were above the rock face and settled down for the night. Again their dinner consisted of flour soup.

Early the next morning, the men came to a frozen tarn, which they named Lake Mary. They crossed the ice to the opposite shore, where a little swell of ground arose, from the top of which they could see another lake; this they christened Lake Margaret. They assumed the barrier between the lakes was "the divide, or height of land" but they were mistaken, although the divide was only a stone's throw away.

After nearly five months, the Press Expedition had finally reached the central divide of the Olympic Mountains, the watershed between streams flowing north and streams flowing south. The men crossed the ice of the second lake and headed down the canyon, making rapid progress because everything was covered with compact snow. Early that morning they came to a huge rock, and through a hole in the snow they had their first sight of water running south. After sampling it, the men concluded that it tasted better than the Elwha. As the men stood, gazing at the little brook, the dogs flushed a bear from a clump of trees. Seizing their guns, the men gave chase and shot it.

They could scarcely believe their luck. They now had fat! They had lived exclusively on flour for a week, and little besides flour for several weeks. Understandably, "the prospects of grease seemed a delirious dream." They skinned the bear in record time and soon were frying the liver and slabs of fat. Because they were starved for it, they drank the grease as fast as they could fry it out.

Christie decided to adopt the Indian custom of camping beside the kill. Now that they had meat, the need to hurry was alleviated, and they could take time to explore. Barnes left at once to ascend Mount Seattle, which overlooked the camp, and by late afternoon had climbed two-thirds of the way to the summit. He completed the ascent the following morning, climbing to "a kind of thin ridge or saddle, which connected two sharp unscalable spires of rock, which constituted the actual double summit of the mountain." The view was glorious, the morning sunlight sweeping over mountain ranges as far as he could see. He admired the panorama, photographed it, then worked on his chart.

During his absence, the other men had consumed the bear, and shot another. Shortly after Barnes returned, Hayes spotted a third bear and it, too, was dispatched.

When they broke camp on the divide, the men headed down the Quinault on snowshoes, but when the river emerged from its snow cover they were forced to the sidehills. Generally, the travel was downhill, an agreeable change, but the terrain was steep and rough, broken by slides and obstructed by windfalls and thick undergrowth. The river grew larger, and now and then they came across bare places where winter's snow had disappeared. Most of the way led through a deep, gloomy gorge, and they had to cross numerous side canyons. Because they were on the windward side, the brush grew more rank, the ground was wetter, and rain was frequent. When they were about halfway down the valley, the men became puzzled by the outlook ahead. Following a stream in such dense woods, hemmed in by steep hills, was like "exploring a dark rat hole," and they could see only a few yards in any direction, while overhead the foliage shut out the sky.

During the fourth day, the men noted that the river had changed direction and was flowing eastward. This caused them much concern, because they were determined to exit the mountains via the Quinault, which flowed southwest. They now suspected they had missed the Quinault when they crossed the divide. If so, they were following another river, one that perhaps flowed to Hood Canal, which was not their destination. But they were getting into game country again and were lucky enough to kill an elk. That morning all they had left was twenty-five pounds of flour, so the change in fortune made them optimistic; they felt that with the new supply of meat they could cross over to the Quinault, if it became necessary.

With packs replenished, they resumed the journey. The

valley was snow-free at last, the afternoon warm and sunny. The river now turned definitely westward, and they were relieved of their anxiety. The expedition's troubles and hardships appeared to be over.

About noon on May 17, the men arrived at the juncture of the Quinault's two forks, and they came upon a trapper's cabin, the first sign of civilization since they had left the lower Elwha many weeks before. The river was now large and broad. That night the explorers used the last of their flour to make soup, but they still had enough meat for two days.

Sunday, May 18, was the day "long looked forward to, of meeting white men and getting a taste of civilization." But it was also the day the Press Expedition suffered its greatest misfortune. The men were weary of struggling through the dense jungle, and they noted that the Quinault had flowed smooth and quiet for several miles, its banks and channel free of drift timber. They decided to build a raft, and were working on it when a white man and two Indians appeared in a canoe. The settler was F. S. Antrim of Aberdeen, Washington. He told them Quinault Lake was eight miles distant, said he had a well-stocked cabin at the lake's head, and invited them to help themselves. He was going upriver but would return in a day or so. He then left them to their raft building. The men finished the raft quickly, loaded it, and soon they were gliding down the river. The stream was gentle, and the men congratulated themselves that an early ending of their journey awaited.

The Olympics had one last test to make of the men's "abundance of grit and manly vim." The craft rounded a sharp bend; the river gathered itself into a swift, narrow channel, and swept toward the right bank, where it rushed beneath a large pile of driftwood. The men attempted to save the raft and their packs, but they could do little. When the raft struck the drift pile, two men jumped to the logs and were safe; at the same instant, water poured over the raft, sweeping away two men, the dogs, and all the baggage. Christie, who was standing and had the steering oar, stayed with the raft and managed to rescue one of the men swept away; the other, Barnes, then surfaced downstream, clutching the pack that held the expedition's records.

Two men were now on one side of the river, three on the other. They had lost everything except the contents of the one pack and the clothes they wore. Gone were the guns, ammunition, bear skins, fishing tackle, and all but a few of the mineral specimens they had collected. Many little curios, such as bear and elk teeth, were also lost.

But most important of all, the pack they saved contained the trip records—the journals, negative films, and the map they had made of the Olympics. Everyone was safe, including the dogs; that was another major consolation. Eventually, the

divided expedition started out once again on foot. The thick brush impeded their travel, and they had no food. The men camped that night without shelter. Rain fell, and by morning they had long been wet to the skin.

Antrim came by again, and took them to the lake in his canoe. The rain stopped, the clouds rolled back, and the sun shone. The men saw numerous piles of driftwood, and it quickly became evident that rafting down the river would have been impossible.

When the party reached Antrim's cabin, the men directed their first attention to his stores. Their meal consisted of biscuits, potatoes, broiled ham, and baked salmon, mingled with the aroma of coffee. But Antrim's treasures did not end there. He had butter, sugar, syrup, condensed milk, mustard, and pickles. The feast was of long duration, but somewhat hastened toward the end by the men's desire to smoke, they having obtained tobacco from the Indians.

The explorers left about two o'clock, and now that they were in touch with civilization, they were anxious to get home. They had lived nearly six months in primitive wilderness with the sky for a roof. Taking their places in the little canoe, they ventured

James H. Christie and Robert B. Hitchman, August 1937, Vernon, B.C. (Photo courtesy Robert B. Hitchman)

out upon the tranquil waters of Quinault Lake. They crossed it quickly, then glided down the lower Quinault. They camped about nine miles below the lake, and again prepared "another wonderful feast" from Antrim's stores.

The next day the men were astir before daylight and on their way at four o'clock. About ten o'clock they reached the Indian Agency at the river's mouth. Here they hired a team to transport them down the beach. The party arrived at Oyhut shortly after dark, boarded a sloop for Grays Harbor, and arrived in Aberdeen two hours past midnight on May 21, "having by 22 hours of continuous travel made a distance of 60 miles."

The few people who happened to be near the wharf when the Press Expedition arrived "were surprised, not to say startled, by the appearance of five human beings clothed in tattered garments, bare headed except [for] a strip of handkerchief or other cloth around their foreheads, dusty, [with] unkempt beard and flowing hair like wild men of the woods. They were sunburned and tanned as by long exposure, and no feverish gold hunter of '49 could have presented a more utter absence of the outward civilization of man than did these strangers. Following them were three shaggy dogs, such as might have trained with the Esquimaux or dragged the sledge of Arctic explorers. As quietly as they came

these strange beings sought refuge from public gaze in one of our hotels, declining to talk or say who or what they were, and conducted themselves as though they knew their own business and proposed to attend to it."

Because of the late hour, the explorers had difficulty obtaining accommodations, but when they at last touched real beds, "it was a luxury to be appreciated." When they arose the next morning, they learned that news of their return had preceded them. They received telegrams of congratulation from the *Seattle Press* and from many friends. They had interviews in their rooms with various merchants, with barbers, and with a photographer who took their group picture. When at last they were able to resume a civilized appearance, they hardly recognized themselves. Only their bronzed faces remained to remind them of what they had been through.

After two days of badly needed rest, the men traveled to Seattle. Their arrival at the steamer's wharf ended their journey. Their exploration of the Olympics had been completed. All that remained to be done, after the party disbanded, was the reporting of the expedition's adventures by Christie and Barnes. Their accounts of the first known crossing of the Olympics were published in the July 16, 1890, edition of the *Seattle Press*.

5

Wickersham's Wanderings

URING THE SUMMER OF 1889, JAMES Wickersham, a Tacoma probate judge, organized a private trip to explore the Olympic Mountains, with Lake Cushman the destination. Accompanied by Charles E. Taylor and John M. Palmer, he left Tacoma in early June, "and no boys off for a lark ever looked after guns, fishing tackle, ammunition and knives with more real pleasure." The men traveled to Hood Canal via the upper waterways of Puget Sound, making a couple of overland portages.

The adventurers were impressed during the journey down Hood Canal to Union City. "A vast unbroken wilderness stretched away at either hand," Wickersham recorded in his notebook, "while the deep clear waters of the Canal were unruffled, except by the gentle breasts of gull and ducks." Overhead, a large, white-headed eagle winged its way from shore to shore, and on the surface a seal stuck his head out of the salt water and looked at them in mild surprise, then doubled up like a jackknife and disappeared. "How quiet everything is," Wickersham noted, "No human voice, no human sounds—no signs of civilization—only high woody shores and solitude."

At Union City, Charles W. Joynt, the judge's boyhood chum, became the fourth member of the party. He worked for the *Buckley Banner*, and was presently courting one of Wickersham's sisters. Union City consisted of a hotel and store, an old wharf, a schoolhouse, and two or three ancient dwellings. The settlement had a spectacular view of the Olympic Mountains across the blue waters of Hood Canal. A logger named John McReavy was the town's only businessman. He kept "a large supply of logging outfits and everything needed by that class of people." He also ran "the hotel and saloon, democratic politics and other small matters."

Union City was the last place to obtain outdoor gear and provisions, and here the men purchased a full supply of "everything

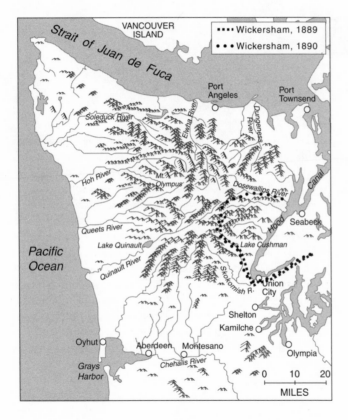

used in camping, fishing and hunting, both meat and drink." The storekeeper's brother then took them across Hood Canal to Hoodsport, where the trail to Lake Cushman began.

Hoodsport was merely one house occupied by the John V. Finch family. At this point the men made up packs, and the party split temporarily. Two men elected to go no farther that day and remained at Finch's overnight; Wickersham and the other man headed for the lake. They started late in the afternoon, and by dark had gone only four or five miles, when they came upon a settler "holding down a ranch" in the deep forest. His name was John Dow, and his log house was their lodging place that night. With true Western hospitality, he set out the best in the house for them, and they were pleasantly surprised to find he was "a man of more than ordinary intelligence. He had a small library, many newspapers and magazines, and talked of matters of public interest in an appreciative way." His wife of mixed parentage (half Indian, half white) was "neatness itself" and they enjoyed a good supper, a clean bed, and a warm breakfast. They resumed their journey before sunrise, but were overtaken by the other men before they reached Lake Cushman. The men "enjoyed the walk through the great virgin forest, reaching to the lake, and yet untouched by fire or axe, and only traversed by one foot trail—used, however, as a horse trail at times but extremely rough." Dow's house was the only one along the trail with the exception of two small, deserted cabins that had been built to "prove up on claims."

The men had their first view of the North Fork Skokomish when they reached a point about a mile below the lake. They arrived at the lake at noon and noted that it was not large—about a mile and a half long, perhaps half as wide. The lake appeared to be merely a bulge or enlargement of the river, which flowed into it on the northwest side, then out the south end. Mile-high Mount Ellinor pierced the sky to the north, and on the lake's western side a spur came down to the water's edge. A splendid forest of fir and cedar extended from the lake to Hood Canal; however, according to Wickersham, it had all been fraudulently acquired by a timber company.

The men crossed the lake in a dugout canoe and erected their tent "in a magnificent grove of cottonwood trees" near "the inflowing Skokomish river." They then "dispersed, each to hunt and fish and enjoy life as it best suited him." They caught numerous trout, and ate "many a fine skillet of crisp fish."

Two or three years before, a man named Albert A. Rose had come to the lake, "settled on the flowery meadow between the forked mouths of the Skokomish," and hewed out a home on unsurveyed land. However, he contracted smallpox and died, leaving his widow and children the only residents of the region. Now, however, the widow had a man named Windhoffer in her employ—"a big lout of a fellow" who was "making love to her and working as little as possible." Wickersham added another cynical comment in his notebook: "Like many another fool woman she can see charms in him that no one else can see—verily love is blind—and if he don't propose soon she will."

The couple had two canoes on the lake, but they charged a big price to use them, "and between selling eggs to prospectors and raising garden and stock," they made a pretty good living. Rose had accumulated quite a band of sheep, cattle, and horses, and Wickersham surmised that Windhoffer had his eye on these as well as on the widow.

Because they wanted to know more about the mountains than they could see from the lake, Wickersham and Joynt decided to go up the river as far as possible in one day, then return the next. According to the settlers, no one had ever gone more than a few miles beyond the lake, "and no one had any idea of the character of the country a day's march into the interior," but rumor had it that the center of the Olympics was a level plateau from whence flowed several rivers, the Skokomish among them. But again, no one had actually viewed this country.

Wickersham and Joynt left camp at six a.m. on June 8, each carrying his gun, ammunition, hunting knife, compass, and enough food to last two days. The latter consisted of crackers or hardtack and canned beef, with salt in case they killed game. They had a good supply of matches, but did not take blankets or bedding with them.

The men followed the river through dense growths of fir and cedar, and after about a mile came to the home of Whitley, a settler who hailed from Missouri. He was married, had a wife, one child, a mother-in-law, "and a dozen dogs." The family lived in a neat log cabin and had succeeded in clearing a tiny garden spot. Leaving the rancher some of their superfluous clothing, the enthusiastic explorers headed north, up the valley, "following a dim trail through the woods." Whitley walked with them a short distance, and they were pleased with his appearance. Wickersham described him as "a typical frontiersman—a bee hunter, bear fighter and a hunter of deer and elk. Tall, strong and muscular, wears a broad brimmed yellow hat, spotted with bear grease—slow of speech but frank of manner, and a great 'terbacker chawer.'"

A mile or so above the canyon the river bed was choked with enormous boulders, the stream broken by rapids and falls, an impassable torrent. Beyond the rapids were three new but unoccupied "log shanties" set in small clearings. No other signs of human life were evident. The explorers strapped on their gear tightly, "took a last look at civilization and plunged into the forest—without path or guide, above any known point." As they proceeded, they named almost everything they saw, but none of the names are used today.

They followed elk trails for miles "through a dense forest skirting the banks of the river, with no evidence that human steps had ever before gone that way." At times they scaled high, rocky cliffs that were almost perpendicular, then again found themselves struggling through windfalls and boulders covered with moss eighteen and twenty inches thick. Had the elk not worked a trail through these barriers with their heavy, sharp hooves during their semi-annual migrations from the upper to the lower ranges for many years, it would have deterred explorers with stronger wills than they had from making the attempt.

The men had gone about five miles beyond the lake when they reached a point where "masses of red stone" extended upward from the river, and they were forced to climb in order to proceed. Now they discovered that others had preceded them— they passed by "an old camp" where the names of three men and the date July 12, 1887, were written upon a blazed tree. They stopped for lunch at a place where the river fell about one

Lake Cushman about the turn of the century (Photo by A. H. Barnes, courtesy Special Collections Division, University of Washington Libraries)

hundred feet in a half mile, forming a series of picturesque rapids. Here the stream was filled with enormous rocks. The terrain became increasingly rugged, but the men arrived safely at the head of the gorge, only to find there was "another mountain chasm" just beyond. They would not have been able to proceed except that they chanced upon "a plain and well beaten elk trail."

Late that afternoon the men rounded the mountain, and the path led them to the top of a small peak from where they could see, directly north, "what appeared to be an opening in the mountains." Because this was the direction in which they desired to proceed, they descended, crossed the river and headed "in a northerly direction." As they worked their way down, they noted the stream that "bore away to the west" was not the Skokomish, but a tributary. They stopped to have supper at the creek's mouth, each man partaking of one hardtack with some canned meat. They had not observed any game during the day except ducks, grouse and squirrels, none of which they attempted to kill. Joynt now tried his hand at fishing, but he was not successful. The men noted that the Skokomish flowed from the northwest, and they decided to make camp shortly. Because the terrain at the creek's mouth was unsuitable, they crossed the stream on a makeshift

James Wickersham (Photo courtesy Special Collections Division, University of Washington Libraries, neg. no. 14349)

bridge of poles and rocks, and with considerable difficulty climbed the opposite wall. After tramping about a half mile to the northwest, they had a good view up the valley. "Looking into the deep and hazy distance to the north," Joynt wrote, "we discovered that the oft-repeated legend of the Indians was not altogether a myth, but in all probability a fact. We could plainly discern that a large crater-like table-land lay to the north of us, bounded on the south and north by a backbone or summit of a few hundred feet high."

The men descended a bit into the canyon of the West Branch, about a hundred yards above its junction with the main river. After attempting to view "the wild and raging waters of this gorge," they climbed about halfway up the bluff, built their campfire, "and prepared for a night's rest."

The larger of the two streams at this point was the main Skokomish. The smaller one, the West Branch, was impassable for even a trout. The stream was full of huge boulders, and confined in a narrow channel between great walls of rock, and down this narrow passage it thundered and plunged, creating falls and rapids in its "never ceasing hurry to the sea below." They could neither ascend nor descend "without climbing entirely out of the gorge." Wickersham felt that the West Branch needed a name, and because his genial friend Charles W. Joynt was one of the first discoverers, he named it Joynt River.

Their campsite was too steep for comfort, "and only by lying against a fallen log" could they maintain a place on the ground

at all. Gravity tended to drag them downhill, and without the assistance of the log as a barricade it was "extremely difficult to lie in one spot long." They kept the fire going all night, and by wrapping themselves in their rubber coats they managed to sleep fairly comfortably.

The next morning, Sunday, June 9, the men began their return journey, having decided that traveling northward another half day would not add much to their knowledge. They could see about fifteen miles of the main river, and the low pass due north convinced them that a road could be built that far. After breakfast en route, they struck an elk trail going in their direction, and they followed it to the summit of a little mountain about two thousand feet high. The top was a weathered rock devoid of vegetation except for mosses and a few wildflowers, with "plenty of elk sign." Here they rested and viewed the country. They were surrounded by lofty peaks except to the southeast, where the Skokomish broke through the foothills on its way to the sea. They could hear the river's roar coming up from below. A fringe of timber above their perch provided welcome shade, while a gentle south wind cooled their blood, which had been "heated by the laborious climb to the summit. Our enjoyment of this novel situation is exquisite," Wickersham wrote, "for it is my first visit to even a minor mountain summit."

By the time they reached Lake Cushman, the men were "weary and worn out," having subsisted for two days on hardtack, canned beef, and water, but they felt that they "had seen a country heretofore unknown to white men." Their companions were glad to see them safely back, and after a good supper they retired "and had a full night's rest under a blanket." Two days later, the men left Lake Cushman and walked to John Finch's. When they arrived in Hoodsport, they learned that a great fire had devastated the business section of Seattle. They crossed over to Union City, "and after a good night's rest took the stage for Shelton," and then made their way by steamer to Tacoma. Their outing in the Olympics had ended.

A year later, the summer of 1890 turned out to be a busy one for explorers. The Olympics swarmed with men bent on unlocking mysteries. Lieutenant Joseph P. O'Neil led the largest party, the Olympic Exploring Expedition, sponsored by the Oregon Alpine Club, and it was headed up Wickersham's valley, the North Fork Skokomish! Not to be outdone, Wickersham and his friends hastened to return, their 1889 trip having whetted their desire to explore further. This time they were accompanied by several other relatives, including women, and the expedition was pretty much a family affair. Backed by two newspapers, the *Buckley Banner* and the *Tacoma News*, the group became known as the Banner Party. This expedition was the first organized group to explore the headwaters of the Duckabush and descend the Dosewallips, but it achieved this distinction because it followed hot on O'Neil's heels and used the trail he cut through the primitive forest. By traveling without pack animals and not having to build a trail, the Wickersham party was able to move more rapidly. Accordingly, it quickly overtook and passed the military expedition.

The rivalry at this time—eight months after Washington Territory had become Washington State—between the various exploring parties was intense. The *Buckley Banner,* for example, belittled O'Neil, alleging he would travel westward through a district that had often been visited before, whereas (the newspaper claimed) Wickersham's schedule called for his party to journey northward "through the heart of the Olympics," penetrating a district that no one had ever gone through. The newspaper said that one member of the Banner Party was "an old mineral prospector" who intended to collect numerous ore samples. The expedition would also take many photographs of the country. As a matter of fact, the party would leave all pleasure behind at Lake Cushman, and "take up a line of march prepared for hard and thorough work."

Numbering about a dozen people (only half of whom intended to go beyond Lake Cushman), the Banner Party left Tacoma on July 19, 1890, and traveled via steamer to Olympia and Shelton, then by stage to Union City. Here they purchased the food needed

for their trip, because this was the last store upon their route into the mountains. The items acquired "consisted of 20 pounds of flour to the man, 10 pounds of meal, 5 pounds of salt, 15 pounds of bacon, 3 cans of baking powder, 6 tin plates, 3 tin cups, fish hooks, chewing gum, French harp and tin whistle, and a long-handled frying pan." In addition they also packed "3 blankets, guns, ammunition, knives, kodak, knapsacks, 100 feet of rope and extra clothing."

A steamer conveyed the party across Hood Canal to Hoodsport, "a new town just starting up on the west side." Here they met Lieutenant O'Neil, who offered to carry their packs on his mules as far as his camp on the Skokomish River. He also loaned them one little black mule to assist the ladies as far as Lake Cushman. Everything went well until they were nearly halfway to the lake, when the mule disturbed a nest of yellow jackets. The animal reared and kicked, causing the rider to lose her balance and fall. The men caught the mule and loaded small bundles upon her; the party resumed the march and reached the lake at ten o'clock that night, "having traveled by stage, steamer, muleback, and afoot from Shelton to that point since breakfast—a distance of 25 miles." They then canoed across the lake to a settler's house.

Ida Robbins Finch, Hoodsport pioneer (Photo courtesy Finch's granddaughter Wenonah Sharpe)

The half-dozen people in the party who planned to go beyond Lake Cushman consisted of three men and three women. The men, Wickersham, Joynt, and Taylor, had been on the 1889 trip and knew what to expect. The women were the judge's wife, Deborah Susan Bell Wickersham, and his sisters, Clyde Wickersham and May Taylor. Clyde was the fiance of Joynt, editor of the *Buckley Banner*, and May had just married Taylor.

The couple had "resolved to make this Olympic trip their bridal tour," and they had joined the party the day they were married. Consequently, they had "the unique experience" of spending their honeymoon "tramping more than a hundred miles through an unexplored mountain range."

Upon leaving Lake Cushman, Wickersham followed the miners' trail (which O'Neil had improved) to Fisher's Bluff, then utilized the mule trail cut by the soldiers. Subsequently, on July 23, the Banner Party arrived at O'Neil's Camp Five, near Jumbo's Leap. Here they were royally entertained, the troopers not yet having read the *Buckley Banner* article that belittled the lieutenant. The soldiers invited them to lunch, and the camp took on "more the appearance of a parlor scene than an African jungle," as the guests seated themselves around the campfire. "Our supplies being of the coarse substantial type," Private Fisher wrote, "I was somewhat embarrassed for the ladies as they sat down to lunch." He was soon relieved, however, "by seeing them manipulate the rusty implements as they lay into the bear meat & beans with the grace of old soldiers." The Banner Party then crossed Jumbo's Leap via the footlog and camped for the night on the opposite side. The soldiers "heartily sympathized with the ladies and would have rejoiced to have seen them turn back from their undertaking, well knowing what lay before them." They concluded, however, that the men were experienced in mountain travel and "had been this far before upon elk trails." The mules could not negotiate these paths until the logs had been cut out, and the swampy swales brushed over or detoured around.

The mail arrived, one of the troopers having returned from a trip to Lake Cushman, and O'Neil's men were surprised to learn—through the columns of the press—that they were "out upon a pleasure trip, traveling elk trails, living upon the fat of the land." Both soldiers and scientists felt aggrieved: "We who had patched our clothes by the light of a pine knot in our eagerness to make every day a full one!" When they discovered that the remarks had been fathered by the Banner Party, their luncheon guests who were just now setting up camp across the creek, they immediately focused their attention on "the masculine sex of their party, who, in their weakness, had pricked us with the pen. However, we passed it by, well knowing that our work would mark our course with brands more lasting than printer's ink or serpent's sting. Perhaps our feelings were wounded in this attempt to misinform the public."

The members of the Banner Party arose early the next morning

Members of the John V. Finch family in front of their Hoodsport home (Photo courtesy Robert V. Finch)

The lake the Banner Party called Lake Darrell is known today as Lake LaCrosse (Photo by the author)

and were engaged in pistol practice when the soldiers, overlooking their shortcomings, brought them hot coffee. Wickersham and his companions thanked them, "did justice to the menu," then headed up the North Fork. They had no further contact with O'Neil's expedition.

Beyond Jumbo's Leap, the Banner Party, having leaped past O'Neil, did not have the benefit of a man-made path to follow, and therefore took to elk trails whenever that was possible. The first major obstacle the explorers encountered was the West Branch of the Skokomish, the stream Wickersham had named Joynt River the previous summer. The party camped overnight on its banks, above the place where the stream plunged over a precipice, creating a picturesque waterfall. (When O'Neil's men arrived a few days later, they called the cascades Honeymoon Falls, in honor of Charles and May Taylor, the Banner Party's newlyweds.)

Upon reaching the divide rising between the Skokomish and the Duckabush, the Banner Party explorers saw tarns below, on the north slope, with snow and ice still floating upon them. After its contact with O'Neil, the Banner Party began naming its camps for various members of the military expedition—O'Neil, Linsley, Henderson, Bretherton, and Church, in that order. At the point where they crossed the divide, the women "fulfilled their promise to Lieutenant O'Neil" by placing upon a "pinnacle of snow" a flag that bore the figure 14 in honor of the Fourteenth Infantry. (When O'Neil saw the banner a few days later, he did not remove it but left it as "a monument to the pluck and bravery of . . . the first ladies to cross the Olympic range.")

The Banner Party descended to a little plateau and camped near one of two tarns that sparkled in the sunlight. They carved an inscription on a tree: "Banner Expedition, July 29, 1890. Soldier Camp. James Wickersham, Deborah Wickersham, Clyde Wickersham, Chas. E. Taylor, May W. Taylor, Charles W. Joynt. From Lake Cushman to Port Angeles."

Beyond this camp they descended to the Duckabush River, then headed upstream to the parklike country at its headwaters by following well-beaten game trails. Eventually they reached, just a week or two ahead of O'Neil, "the height of land in the central plateau" from which issued four large rivers—the Skokomish, Duckabush, Dosewallips, and East Fork Quinault.

Having reached the heart of the mountains, the party spent several days encamped in the high meadows, leisurely enjoying the country and examining the topography, flora, and fauna. They were impressed on the hot July days by the cascades that tumbled down the steep slopes; by the meadowland where grasses and flowers grew in wild abandon; by the scattered clumps of conifers; by the sparkling streams that flowed from the melting snowfields; and, lastly, by an old glacier "covered with boulders and rubble from avalanches." This lovely stretch of subalpine meadowland appeared to have never known the trod of a human foot prior to the Banner Party's visit. The basin was, in fact, "one vast solitude." But the days of isolation were coming to an end. The Banner Party had brought civilization to the interior Olympics, and O'Neil's large expedition arrived shortly afterward.

The Banner Party discovered a pear-shaped lake in the meadows, and upon it floated "great cakes of ice covered with snow." They named it Lake Darrell, but a week or two later, two of O'Neil's scouts called it Lake of the Holy Cross because "the trunk of a once large tree overlooked it, and upon either side of it at right angles there extended a limb, forming a cross which was richly festooned with moss, and whose image was reflected from the calm clear waters beneath."

To see the distant views, the Banner Party climbed up to the divide to the west. This vista point overlooked the Quinault as well as the Duckabush and Dosewallips, revealing a panoramic view. The peaks stretched away "in every direction in tumultuous array, like the storm swept waves of the sea; no well defined range, but a mass of mountain peaks, rough, serrated, and new." Far down the Quinault, they could see a pale band of blue which they took to be the Pacific Ocean; looking eastward, they could discern Hood Canal. When he described the scene, Wickersham waxed eloquent: "Everywhere lie snowbanks, glaciers, flowery meadows, lakes, and groves. Magnificent waterfalls roar and splash down the mountain buttresses, reaching the canyon bottom in fine spray, and with the action of the winds, make music on nature's own aeolian harps. Here music, flowers, birds, sunshine, and spring; there fogs, ice, rocks, and drear winter—every variety of scenery and climate in a few minutes from our high porch."

The climbers noted that the East Fork Quinault began as a "full-fledged river from underneath a glacier." They called it the Quinault Glacier, but it is known today as Anderson Glacier. This was the largest ice field they had observed in the Olympics, but it appeared to be receding. Barren areas that had recently become free of ice indicated that the glacial age was, in the geologic sense, coming to a close in the Olympics.

The glacier occupied "a crater-like cavity" near the summit of a double-peaked mountain between the heads of the Quinault and Dosewallips. The Banner Party called the peak Mount Allyn, but a few weeks later O'Neil named it Mount Anderson, for his commanding officer, Colonel Thomas M. Anderson, and it is so known today. Although high on the mountain's flanks, the glacier was easily approached and explored. The East Fork Quinault

Mount Anderson and Linsley Glacier from Fisher's Notch (Photo by the author)

emerged from its terminus, the river leaping "from its glacial home over 500 feet of mountain wall, striking with a roar on the rocks below."

Almost directly south of Mount Allyn, and seven miles distant, rose another double-peaked mountain, massive and sprawling, between the headwaters of the Quinault, Duckabush, and Skokomish. Wickersham estimated its elevation to be seventy-four hundred feet, which was more than a thousand feet higher than the true altitude. Still, the mountain was precipitous and offered a definite challenge.

The party climbed one of the twin peaks with enthusiasm, but when "rounding its snowy summit," Deborah Susan Bell Wickersham "missed her footing, fell, and rolled down the snow at a frightful velocity." She slid toward a mountain wall that dropped almost vertically for hundreds of feet, and it appeared as if nothing could save her; but the rocks at the precipice's brink arrested her descent. She had no more than regained her equilibrium when her companions named the peak Mount Susan, "with the hope that no future geographer would feel it necessary to change the name." However, it was not to be; the peak's name was changed on several occasions. Less than two weeks later, O'Neil's scouts arrived, and they tentatively identified the peak as Mount Skookum, a Chinook jargon word meaning "big" or "important." Five days later they rechristened it Mount Arline,

after the eldest daughter of Colonel Thomas M. Anderson. Finally, the name was changed again to Mount Steel, to honor Will G. Steel, who helped O'Neil organize his expedition in 1890. Before the turn of the century, however, the double peaks constituting the mountain were given individual names—the higher one became Mount Duckabush, with the name Mount Steel retained for the lower peak.

Life in the high country between Mounts Allyn and Susan proved to be "one continuous surprise." One August night was particularly memorable, and "indeed a change from a comfortable home in the city." The party was encamped at Lake Darrell when, about dusk, storm clouds rolled over the ridge from the Quinault side and settled down, almost instantly changing the weather from summer to winter. "The driving mists, like a blinding snow storm, the shades of falling night, the surrounding snowfields and icebergs in the lake, made an arctic condition that drove us to build a roaring fire of logs. The moisture, however, penetrated our very bones and, being without a tent, we erected a shelter of bark that but poorly protected the three ladies. We were blue, cold, and uncomfortable, without any prospect of rest until daybreak." About ten p.m., however, a north wind "sprang up strong and cold . . . and the clouds went flying away leaving the sky without a blemish, while the north wind rapidly turned the moisture to ice and frost." An hour later the moon appeared over Mount Susan, "and its first bright rays discovered our whole party energetically exercising to keep warm.

"The great meadow, now covered with frost, seemed to be carpeted with diamonds. The moonlight made every crystal on ice or snow, as well as on the waving trees, sparkle and flash like the richest jewels, while the floating icebergs in the lake, the long shadows of the trees, the moonlight on the circle of mountain wall back of us, the distant glaciers, glistening like burnished silver, and the heavens ablaze with a myriad of diamond lights made an August night picture never to be forgotten."

The Banner Party had planned to cross the ranges to the Elwha and follow the river northward to Port Angeles. However, after looking at the Quinault gorge, which would have to be crossed if the explorers were to adhere to their plan, they concluded that the country was too rough. Consequently, they turned their gaze eastward toward Hood Canal, and exited the mountains by first following the ridge between the Duckabush and Dosewallips, then descending to the latter and following it to Hood Canal. Here they caught a steamer which took them back to civilization. They had been in the mountains three weeks, often forcing their way through thick undergrowth, clambering over fallen trees, wading torrents, sloshing through swamps, climbing mountains, and they often "slept above clouds." The last week had been the most

difficult, and they had subsisted in the style of the Press Expedition, on cakes made with flour and water. Despite the hardships, they had gone a considerable distance into the southeastern Olympics, and they were the first group to traverse the West Fork of the Dosewallips from its source to its mouth.

The Banner Party was more a family adventure or summer outing than an organized exploring expedition. Nevertheless, its members traveled by foot a great many miles, most of them over terrain where man-made trails were nonexistent. The trip must have been especially difficult for the women, clothed as they were. Wickersham wrote: "Our ladies dressed for the trip in soft felt hats, blue ducking short skirts, blue ducking overalls, drawn tight around the ankle, and heavy leather shoes, with soles filled with hobnails. The men dressed similarly, all wearing rough, heavy, strong clothing." Although Wickersham referred to the skirts as short, they would not have been so considered if judged by today's standards. Photographs taken by the party show the skirts reaching halfway between knees and ankles and, in some instances, practically sweeping the ground.

Wickersham's explorations resulted in one major, far-reaching contribution: He recommended that the best part of the Olympic Mountains be set aside as a national park. His is believed to be the first proposal advocating the creation of a national park on the Olympic Peninsula. He made it in letters dated November 3

Members of the Banner Party pose in the Olympics, 1890
(Reproduced from *The Living Wilderness* [Summer-Fall 1961])

and 8, 1890, which he wrote to two publishing companies. Then, in April 1891, he sent an article about the Olympics to the Century Publishing Company, but the story was not accepted. Finally, on July 21, 1891, he sent his article and maps describing "a proposed Olympic National Park" to Major John W. Powell, Director of the United States Geological Survey.

At that time, Wickersham pointed out, no national park existed in Idaho, Montana, Nevada, Oregon, Washington, or Alaska. Everywhere the virgin forests were being destroyed, the wildlife killed. He therefore felt that a national park should be established on the public domain at the headwaters of the rivers flowing out of the Olympics. He suggested a park thirty miles wide from north to south, forty miles from east to west, thus comprising twelve hundred square miles, or 768,000 acres, making it one-third the size of Yellowstone National Park, which had been established in 1872. Such a park would include the highest parts of the Olympics, the headwaters of the rivers, the glaciers, the loftiest peaks, and, probably most important of all, the ranges of elk, deer, and bear. He also suggested including Lakes Cushman, Quinault, and Crescent, but his sketch map of the proposed park excludes them.

Wickersham thought that the president should withdraw the proposed region from disposal under the public land laws, and set it apart as a reservation. No surveyed lands lay within the proposed boundaries, and no private rights had been acquired; thus, creating the park would not involve withdrawing agricultural lands from settlement. The foothills were covered with dense forests which extended, along the rivers, far into the interior. Except for the California redwoods, probably the heaviest forest growth in North America was found here, untouched by fire and axe, and far enough from tidewater that reserving it would not cripple private enterprise. A national park would serve the two-fold purpose of "a great pleasure ground" and a means of protecting the forests and wildlife.

The Olympics, Wickersham noted, were "a veritable hunter's and fisherman's paradise." Elk, deer, bear, cougar, wildcat, beaver, and marmot were numerous; the streams were filled with trout and salmon. He estimated the elk population at three hundred, and thought that without protection they would soon disappear. "Something should be done to protect them," he wrote, "and nothing would be more effectual than a national park."

Lieutenant O'Neil made a similar statement shortly afterward, when he, too, recommended creation of a national park in the Olympics. We do not know which man, Wickersham or O'Neil, was the first to get the *idea* of an Olympic National Park. Although documentary evidence does not exist to sustain it, the probability is high that the two men arrived at the idea simultaneously when they met on the Skokomish River in July 1890. At that time they undoubtedly exchanged ideas and information, and they probably discussed the future of the Olympics.

Wickersham, after serving as a probate judge and Tacoma city attorney, and member of the state legislature at one time, moved to Alaska in 1900, where he became a federal judge. He was also a delegate to Congress. He advocated the creation of Mount McKinley National Park, the establishment of the first Alaskan legislature, and statehood for Alaska. He also made the first recorded attempt to climb Mount McKinley.

In 1896, before he relocated to Alaska, Wickersham was invited to join the Mazamas, an Oregon mountaineering club which had risen like a phoenix from the ashes of the defunct Oregon Alpine Club. He accepted only on condition that his wife be permitted to join also, because she was a much better mountaineer than he, and she had frequently led the way when climbing the snow-capped peaks in the Olympics, never before reached by human foot.

6

The Alpine Club Expedition

LIEUTENANT JOSEPH P. O'NEIL, WHO HAD had to cut short his Olympic explorations when he was ordered to Fort Leavenworth, Kansas, in the late summer of 1885, returned to Vancouver Barracks, Washington Territory, on August 8, 1887, having completed his training at the School of Application for Infantry and Cavalry. Six weeks later, Will G. Steel and other climbers founded the Oregon Alpine Club, and they elected the lieutenant to be the organization's secretary. About a year afterward, the new club began advocating that a "scientific expedition" explore the Olympic Mountains, and O'Neil decided to complete the explorations he had begun in 1885.

Brigadier General John Gibbon, commanding the Department of the Columbia, approved the project, and the club appointed O'Neil and Steel to perfect the arrangements. The club would provide the scientific staff and finance the operation; the Army would furnish the leader, enlisted men, and pack train. The party would thus be a mix of military and civilian personnel.

The expedition, billed as the most important sent out by the government since Oregon's pioneer days, would examine the mountains in the summer of 1890. The Olympic Exploring Expedition—or OEE, as it was commonly referred to—would cross the Olympics from east to west, constructing a pack train trail and exploring as it did so. The intent was to obtain accurate, detailed information about the country. The scientists planned to report on the geology, flora, fauna, and ornithology, and also intended to map the region and describe the topography. The expedition's highlight was to be an ascent of Mount Olympus, with placement of a copper box and register upon the summit.

O'Neil had the entire summer at his disposal. Now twenty-seven years of age, he looked forward to a break from the monotonous routine of garrison life. The stories he had heard led him to believe that great mineral wealth awaited discovery, and he stated that possibly this made him more anxious to explore than the prospect of adventure in an unknown land.

When the party was organized, the lieutenant traveled to

Puget Sound to make preparations for their journey. This resulted in his decision to approach the Olympics from the southeast, via the waterway known as Hood Canal, and cross the ranges to the Pacific Ocean. He was told that a trail ran from Hood Canal to Lake Cushman, about six or seven miles inland. This lake, lying at the base of the mountains, was hidden by the foothills, but it had been known for forty years, although the country beyond was largely unexplored.

O'Neil decided to set up a depot camp at the lake and transport the expedition's supplies from Hood Canal to that point. He then procured a scow large enough to accommodate the party, and engaged a steamer to tow the scow from Port Townsend to Hoodsport, where the trail began.

The lieutenant's plan called for going up the North Fork Skokomish to its headwaters. He would then attempt to locate the end of his 1885 trail, and proceed westward, coming out at whatever point the expedition could attain. He intended to keep most of his men busy cutting a trail over which pack animals could travel, while two or three scouts went ahead to search for the best route. Later, after the expedition had penetrated the mountains for some distance, small exploring parties, carrying a

Will G. Steel, who helped O'Neil organize the Olympic Exploring Expedition in 1890 (Photo courtesy Donald Onthank, The Mazamas)

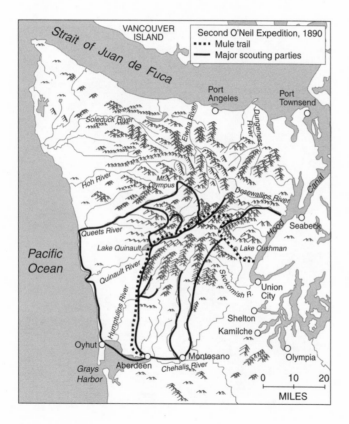

week's provisions, would go forth in various directions and explore the adjacent territory. When they returned, these parties would report their findings in detail. O'Neil felt that this procedure would enable the men to thoroughly explore about sixteen hundred square miles.

The orders formally authorizing O'Neil to reconnoiter the Olympics were published on June 20, 1890. Ten soldiers would accompany him. The lieutenant had no problem in securing men willing to go. In fact, they volunteered in large numbers because they were bored with life on a military post. The enlisted men, all from the Fourteenth Infantry, consisted of three sergeants (Franklin W. Yates, William Marsh, and Frederick Haffner) and seven privates (John Bairens, Jacob Kranichfeld, John Hughes, Emanuel Krause, John E. Higgins, Harry Fisher, and John Danton). O'Neil was fortunate, as he had been in 1885, "in procuring one or two good shots, men who with a Springfield carbine could cut the head from a grouse in 50 or 75 yards five times out of six." M. Price, a civilian employed by the Quartermaster Department, was selected to take charge of the pack train. The other civilians comprised the "scientific corps" of the Oregon Alpine Club: Louis F. Henderson, botanist; Nelson E. Linsley, mining engineer, mineralogist, and geologist; and Bernard J. Bretherton, naturalist.

The expedition had a dozen pack mules, plus several dogs,

and it was well equipped with arms, ammunition, guns, and provisions. O'Neil expected the chief article of diet to be game, but should it prove to be scarce the men had ample provisions—such items as flour, hardtack, beans, coffee, sugar, salt, and tea, plus four gallons of spirits to be used only for medicinal purposes. The equipment included a number of tools—axes, hatchets, brush-hooks, picks, mattocks, spades, saws, files, hammers, and a mule-shoeing kit. Firearms were carbines, revolvers, and shotguns. The one non-utilitarian item was the copper box that was destined to be left at the highest elevation reached, presumably the summit of Mount Olympus. The supplies, calculated to last one hundred days, plus the equipment weighed four tons. This would all have to be transported on the backs of the mules. Because everything could not be moved in one trip, relaying would be necessary.

The expedition arrived in Fort Townsend on June 26. After the inevitable delay, everything was ready for departure by July 1, and during the evening the loaded ship headed out into Puget Sound. After an all-night run, the vessel landed "men, mules and merchandise" at Lilliwaup, a landing place on Hood Canal. This was not their destination, but the boat's officers, who had a

Nelson E. Linsley, geologist and mineralogist, OEE (Photo by Frank O. Shaw, reproduced from *Steel Points* [July 1907])

financial interest in Lilliwaup, assured the men that the best trail to Lake Cushman led from Lilliwaup, not Hoodsport. At Lilliwaup, the men and materiel were transferred to small boats, but the mules were forced to swim to shore. Once everything was present on the beach, the men sorted the packs, fed and loaded the mules, then stored the excess provisions at a nearby ranch.

Having been told the lake was only six miles distant, via a good trail, O'Neil planned to camp there that night. However, the trail was in poor condition, and often blocked by windfalls. Rain fell, the mules were unruly; the pack ropes, new and kinky, often became loosened, causing the packs to slip. Several mules rolled down the steep hill near Lilliwaup. These conditions rendered the first day's march the most difficult one of the entire trip. The men spent most of the time extricating mules from mud. Consequently, the pack train did not go more than three or four miles, and the exhausted men were forced to bivouac in a swamp.

The next morning, however, the sun shone brightly, and the men were much charmed when they saw Lake Cushman overshadowed by snow-capped peaks. The lake had been discovered in 1852, and the first settlers had arrived about thirty years later.

Bernard J. Bretherton, naturalist, OEE, with his "collecting gun" (Photo by Walter W. Bretherton, courtesy Alice Bretherton Powell)

O'Neil now went ahead to make arrangements, and secured a large log raft upon which to ferry the party across the lake to Windhoffer's ranch. Here the men set up Camp One. Two days later, Frederic Church visited them and volunteered to accompany the expedition. O'Neil accepted his offer, and the young man was given several assignments: scout, newspaper correspondent, and assistant geologist.

Beyond the ranch, a good trail led upriver for five miles to a miners' camp, the last outpost of civilization. Man-made trails were nonexistent beyond it, and the explorers would be compelled to cut their way through jungled virgin forests.

O'Neil established a strict work schedule. The men ate breakfast at six a.m., then worked steadily until seven P.M., when they had their evening meal. They were given an hour's rest at noon, but this time was generally used in mending the camp outfit, washing clothes, and doing related chores. The cook was always busy, fixing extra lunches in addition to regular meals because detachments of the pack train came and went at all hours. Nevertheless, the men did find time for a little recreation. Although much fatigued when their workday ended, they fished during the evening hours and caught large numbers of trout.

The explorers worked their way upriver. About a half mile beyond the miners' camp, the expedition halted abruptly because a steep bluff rose directly from the river's edge, barring the way.

Left: *Louis F. Henderson, botanist, OEE* (Photo courtesy Walter and Jean Walkinshaw). Right: *William T. Putnam, who operated Cushman House on Lake Cushman* (Photo courtesy William T. Putnam, Jr.)

The men named it Fisher's Bluff, and established Camp Two nearby.

Only a week had gone by since the explorers had left Fort Townsend; the bluff was the first major barrier. The pack train could not avoid it by crossing the river because the stream was too swift to ford. The only possible solution was to build a pathway, at a forty-five degree angle, up and over the bluff, climbing several hundred feet. However, the men set to work diligently and soon accomplished the task.

Before the expedition left Camp Two, all the supplies had been brought up from Lilliwaup, except for some remaining at the ranch. The pack train had taken more than a week to transport everything from Hood Canal to Lake Cushman; henceforth, the packers could use the Hoodsport trail, which proved to be much better than the Lilliwaup route.

Beyond Camp Two, every step was gained by hard work. The men had to clear a way through the tangled forests, grade switchbacks up steep mountainsides, bridge gulches and gorges, and cut ledges across bluffs and spurs, with logs, brush, Devil's club, slide alder, and miry swales succumbing to the assaults of axes, saws, brush-hooks, and shovels. The need for workmen was paramount, and diverted the scientists from botany, geology, and taxidermy to the more irksome tasks of handling saws, axes, picks, and shovels. The continuous rain made this work unpleasant. The clouds clung low on the mountainsides, blotting out the sun, and they so darkened the narrow canyon that they shut out all suggestion of sky.

At Camp Three, O'Neil sent out the first exploration parties. While the main party extended the mule trail up the valley, the scouts examined the adjacent country. In fact, continuous scouting now became the rule, and it involved many tasks—hacking a way through the almost impenetrable undergrowth on the bottomlands, negotiating chasms and canyons, climbing perpendicular cliffs, clearing elk trails, crossing slippery footlogs, and wading through snowdrifts. The expedition was also getting near the haunts of game, and the scouts frequently saw the signs of elk, deer, and bear, although they seldom saw the animals themselves. Nevertheless, the men were optimistic and looked forward to a diet that included elk steaks as well as beans and bacon.

The reconnaissance trips—usually by two or three men—involved the most perilous work the explorers undertook in the Olympics. However, the scouts quickly adjusted to the dangers and hardships. Delays could not be avoided because O'Neil was forced to send parties out in every direction to seek suitable terrain for the trail. Each scouting party went forth equipped with compass, barometer, and route book in order to accurately map the country. When a scouting party returned to the expedition's camp, the men reported what they had discovered, and compiled their map. Consequently, the use of such patrols actually hastened the expedition's progress toward the interior; otherwise, it would have been difficult, if not impossible, to proceed with pack animals.

As the expedition penetrated deeper into the wilderness, the

Members of the OEE in the high country (Photo by Bernard J. Bretherton, courtesy Mary Floyd Kegg and the National Archives and Records Service)

Shelter tent used by the OEE (Photo by Bernard J. Bretherton, courtesy Edward Bretherton)

mountains upon all sides in the distance. This country had to be thoroughly reconnoitered before the trail could be extended; therefore, while the scouts checked out the West Branch, the mules could not be taken beyond Camp Four. O'Neil directed the packer to relay supplies up to this camp, while everyone else went out to look for a way to the divide.

On one scouting trip the men were accompanied by an old hound named Jumbo. When returning to camp, the scouts had to climb down a tree in order to cross the South Branch, here flowing in a steep-walled canyon. The dog could not descend the tree, and he was too large for the men to carry, which left them no alternative but to leave him behind. Not wishing to be abandoned, Jumbo made a desperate leap into the canyon. How he climbed the opposite wall, no one knew, but eventually he returned to camp and became an instant hero. Henceforth, the South Branch was called Jumbo's Leap, "in honor of his daring skill as a mountaineer."

Judging from reports by the scouts, O'Neil concluded it would be impossible to reach the head of the West Branch with a pack train, and that he would have to look elsewhere for a route. About this time, a young man named James R. Church visited the expedition. Although he was not related to Frederic Church, the two had been college classmates, and he had come to visit his friend. Because he had had two years of medical

country became increasingly rugged, the way more difficult. Apparently, the North Fork Skokomish had three major branches (the North, South, and West) that together formed its headwaters. Beyond Camp Four the canyon was narrow, with high schooling, "Dr. Church" was invited to join the party and serve as the expedition's "surgeon."

Beyond Camp Four the men slashed a zigzag trail up the canyon's sides, until they were confronted by Jumbo's Leap, which rushed through a narrow side canyon. This chasm proved to be the second major barrier. Although the scouts had been able to cross, the pack train would have to await the building of a bridge—the most difficult and hazardous work undertaken by the expedition. After failing to bridge the gorge near its confluence with the river, the men found a place upstream where the walls were slanted at a forty-five degree angle. By building inclined approaches, they succeeded in bridging the stream at this point.

Camp Five had been established nearby, and now the Banner Party arrived and remained overnight. O'Neil had met them when he was in Hoodsport, and had given them some assistance.

On July 25, O'Neil dispatched Frederic Church and Bernard Bretherton to explore the South Fork Skokomish. This took longer than they anticipated and they ran out of food, but were assisted near their journey's end by settlers. During their absence

Arline Anderson, daughter of Colonel Thomas M. Anderson. O'Neil named Mount Arline (now Mount Duckabush) in her honor (Photo courtesy Fort Vancouver Historical Society)

Humptulips City, 1890. Harry Fisher is at far right, John Danton fourth from left (Photo by Joseph P. O'Neil, courtesy National Archives)

from camp, the other men extended the mule trail to the West Branch of the North Fork Skokomish. Here they set up Camp Six, near the waterfall they named Honeymoon Falls in honor of the two recently married members of the Banner Party.

The Olympic Exploring Expedition had now overcome two major barriers—Fisher's Bluff and Jumbo's Leap—and had cleared the mule trail about a dozen miles beyond Lake Cushman. Camp Six was located near the foot of the divide. Within a few days, if all went well, the expedition would cross the crest and make a base camp in the heart of the mountains. The lieutenant would then dispatch foot parties in all directions to thoroughly explore the Olympics. Because the scouts reported much snow at the higher elevations, O'Neil decided to make Camp Six the expedition's headquarters for an indefinite time. Everything would be brought up to the depot by the pack train while the scouts searched out the best route across the divide. This was not an easy task, because the Olympics are a chaotic jumble of peaks, ridges, and canyons. The men now realized they would have to inspect almost every foot of the mountains in order to know them. Often, slopes that appeared to be gentle, when viewed from a distance, proved to be extremely rugged beneath the deceptive forest cover. Nevertheless, the expedition was now within striking distance of the "Grand Divide."

Because the West Branch was an impractical route, the scouts attempted to find a way across the divide via the spur they called Deer Mountain. This ridge extended outward from the divide and appeared to provide a direct route to the Quinault River. The men began cutting a trail up this spur, and established Camp Seven, a dry camp where they had to melt snow to obtain water. Again scouts were sent out, but their reports indicated that the pack train could not go westward from this point. The men therefore abandoned Camp Seven and retreated to Camp Six in the river bottom, then sought a route that led northward.

The outlook was not promising, and the men considered sending the mules back to Fort Townsend and packing the loads themselves. All through July they had worked on a trail about a dozen miles long, but they were still confined in a deep, narrow canyon. Although the invention of a flying machine appeared to be the only solution, O'Neil was unwilling to send the pack train back to Hoodsport. He therefore resorted to his former tactics. He suspended trail building and sent everyone except the botanist out to reconnoiter. Unfortunately, Henderson could devote only a limited amount of time to the expedition, and that time had now run out. He said good-bye on August 3 and journeyed homeward. He regretted leaving just as the expedition was approaching the central Olympics, where he had hoped to collect rare plants. So far he had been disappointed, not by lack of variety but because the flora was almost identical with that prevalent in the Cascades.

The scouts now learned that the North Branch was the river's main stem, not merely a tributary, as they had thought. They left it near its head and climbed to the divide between the Skokomish and Duckabush. One scouting party ran into a large elk herd on the north slope and slaughtered a dozen animals. This was far more than the men needed, and most of the meat spoiled and made the explorers sick.

The scouts recommended extending the trail as rapidly as possible to a point near the head of the North Branch, making a camp at that site, with the pack train moving up while the scouts explored farther. They also reported discovery of a feasible route over which the pack train could cross the divide and descend into a valley on the far side.

The Olympic Exploring Expedition had reached a critical point in its exploration of the Olympics. The men had spent six weeks working on trails—first clearing the Lilliwaup and miners' trails, then slashing several miles of new trail through the primeval forest. Simultaneously, they had scouted the neighboring peaks and ridges. Now, after many days, they had discovered a route across the First Divide, a way that could possibly lead them to the Quinault and the Pacific Ocean.

The Skokomish River, with all its branches and tributaries, had been explored, and the men's next work would be in a new watershed. The immediate goal, however, called for extending the trail to some point near the source of the North Fork and establishing several camps along the way. All hands not needed for reconnaissance or pack-train duty were assigned to trail construction. They were busy for a week, during which time they made a new Camp Seven, then Camp Eight.

O'Neil now dispatched Nelson Linsley and Harry Fisher to scout the country beyond the divide. Leaving the North Branch at the site of future Camp Nine, the men climbed to the divide that overlooked the Duckabush, then descended to that river and followed it to its source. Here they explored a beautiful subalpine basin. They were greatly impressed by this "high country," just as the Banner Party had been shortly before, admiring the vistas, lakes, flowers, snowbanks, peaks, and ridges. The scouts named three lakes in the basin—Marmot, Heart, and Holy Cross—then returned to expedition headquarters, which had been moved during their absence to Camp Eight.

The scouts reported they had not been able to find a pack train route that led directly to the Quinault, and O'Neil concluded he had no choice but to cross the First Divide. This, however, would place the expedition on the upper Duckabush, a stream that flowed to Hood Canal, not on the Quinault, which ran to the Pacific. In order to go westward to the sea, the expedition would be compelled to cross the Second or "Grand Divide," the watershed rising between the eastward and westward flowing streams.

Members of the OEE with a bull elk killed by Harry Fisher and Jacob Kranichfeld (Photo by Joseph P. O'Neil, courtesy National Archives)

Eventually, the mule trail was completed to the point where the scouts had left the North Fork Skokomish, and here the explorers made Camp Nine. The men then began constructing a trail up to the First Divide, connecting elk trails wherever that was possible. These game paths guided them over the most feasible terrain, but without improvement they were not good enough to be used by pack animals. In addition, connecting links had to be built to avoid impassable obstacles.

Now "within a day's march of the divide," the expedition was almost out of the dense undergrowth. The elevation at Camp Nine was two thousand feet; the low point in the divide was less than four miles distant, but twenty-five hundred feet higher.

Convinced the pack animals could cross this pass and reach the heart of the mountains, O'Neil was anxious to explore in detail the central area. He called everyone together, complimented the men on what they had accomplished, reminded them that they had overcome many obstacles, and outlined his plan. He told them he was convinced they could reach the Grand Divide with animals and supplies. Once the expedition's stores were cached there, replacements could be obtained by sending the pack train to Hoodsport. This would permit the expedition to explore without fear of starvation, the dread enemy of adventure. The men would be able to work outward from the center in various directions. Should the pack train be unable to go beyond the

Grand Divide, the mules would be returned to Hoodsport, while the men, packing the supplies on their backs, would strike out from the hub in different directions to finish their assignments. Completion of this work would mark the halfway point in the explorations.

O'Neil divided the expedition into four units. He assigned three foot parties to exploring missions, leaving enough men to complete the trail and escort the pack train to a base camp on the Grand Divide. Upon completing their assignments, the foot parties would rendezvous at the base camp and make their reports. Shortly afterward, they would again set forth, exploring to the north and west in the final phase of the expedition's work. The men then retired and "slept their last night under blankets for almost a moon." The next morning the various parties left camp. During their absence, the remaining men extended the trail to the Grand Divide, establishing Camps Ten, Eleven, Twelve, and Thirteen along the way, and Camp Fourteen, the base camp, on the Grand Divide.

One foot party explored the Duckabush and Dosewallips. These men climbed up to the First Divide, crossed to the Duckabush side, and explored that river's headwaters. They then traveled along the divide between the two rivers for some distance. Eventually, they dropped to the Dosewallips and followed that stream to Hood Canal, where they secured passage on a

The Mount Olympus party ascending the Elwha Snowfinger,
September 19, 1890 (Photo by Bernard J. Bretherton, courtesy
National Archives)

steamship to Hoodsport, then returned by way of Lake Cushman
and the expedition's trail to Camp Fourteen.

The second foot party struck south to the head of the South
Fork Skokomish, then crossed over the ridges to explore the
Satsop, Wynoochee, and Whiskahl. The men went on to Grays
Harbor, traveled via public transportation to Hood Canal, and
then walked up the trail to the expedition's base camp.

The third foot party, led by O'Neil, explored the East Fork
Quinault. His men climbed directly from Camp Nine to the
Grand Divide, then descended to the East Fork and followed it
to Quinault Lake. After exploring the Humptulips, this party
proceeded to Grays Harbor, returning by steamer, rail, and stage
to Hoodsport, and traveling up the trail to Camp Fourteen.

During the absence of the exploring parties, the men attached
to the pack train again became discouraged because they were
unable to locate a route the mules could use to cross the Grand
Divide. Everyone except O'Neil thought the pack train would
have to return to Hoodsport. The lieutenant, however, was determined to exit via the Quinault, because he had found a good
route during his reconnaissance. He again returned to his former
tactics and sent every available man out to look for a way. One
of the scouting parties discovered a feasible route via a pass that
was later named for O'Neil. This meant that the expedition could
complete the trail across the Olympics and take the pack train
by way of Grays Harbor. However, time was important; the beginning of autumn was only two weeks away, and the season when
storms raked the mountains was close at hand.

On September 10, Lieutenant O'Neil called everyone together

and outlined what lay ahead. Standing "beneath the twinkling stars and in the glare of the campfire," he told the men he would divide the expedition again, sending out foot parties to complete the explorations while the remaining men escorted the pack train down the Quinault and on to Grays Harbor.

The next day the explorers prepared for the final trip through the mountains. They then moved across the divide, established Camp Fifteen on the Quinault side, and completed the trail from O'Neil Pass down to the Quinault.

On September 12, O'Neil gave the men their final instructions. The expedition was to be divided for the last trip through the mountains. Linsley would lead a large party and explore the northern part of the range, excluding the district O'Neil reconnoitered in 1885. The lieutenant would take charge of another group and explore the rivers to the southward. The remaining men would escort the pack train to Grays Harbor. These assignments were expected to take about a month, and upon their completion everyone except the packers would assemble at Fort Townsend. They would then return to Vancouver Barracks.

Linsley's party had one of the most important assignments of

Nelson Linsley and John Danton during the ascent of "Mount Olympus," September 22, 1890 (Photo by Bernard J. Bretherton, courtesy National Archives)

the entire expedition—to travel north, cross the headwaters of the Elwha, and proceed to Mount Olympus. If possible, the men were to climb the peak and fix upon its summit the Oregon Alpine Club flag and the copper box containing the record book. The party would then split into smaller groups, with the men taking various routes down the Hoh and branches of the Quillayute.

Athena, the "South Peak of Olympus," where the copper box may still repose (Photo by the author)

O'Neil and the remaining men would stick with the pack train until it was sure of getting through. The objective was to get the mules to a tributary of the Quinault where they would meet men, representing the Hoquiam Board of Trade, who were building a trail from Grays Harbor. When contact was made with the Hoquiam party, O'Neil would be free to explore the rivers southwest of Olympus. With several men, he would go part way up the North Fork Quinault, then climb to the divide in order to locate the headwaters of the Queets and Raft rivers. He would then divide the group and send both parties to the sea, one via the Raft, the other via the Queets. Using the trail cut by the Hoquiam people, the pack train would proceed to Quinault Lake, then make its way to Grays Harbor. The mules would be shipped from that point directly to Vancouver Barracks.

The men were directed to carry enough supplies to last a month. Each man put into his packsack twenty-five pounds of flour, one pound of yeast powder, one pound of salt, a half pound of tea, four pounds of sugar, six to eight pounds of bacon, two pounds of smoked meat, and a half pound of chocolate. In addition, they were to carry axes, saws, guns, ammunition, cooking utensils, a half shelter each, "Kodak, copper box, and other necessaries."

"Our packs averaged about 60# each," Fisher wrote, "and we soon discovered that we were loaded to the limit of our abilities. We passed a social evening and turned in upon the grass at several campfires, passing our last night together."

On September 13 the group that was headed for Mount Olympus left Camp Fifteen and descended, via the new trail, to the Quinault, then followed the river to the first important tributary coming in from the north. Here they camped the first night.

During the next few days, the men traveled north to the divide between the Quinault and Elwha, and followed a spur that led them down to the Elwha. Heading up the Elwha, the party climbed through a subalpine basin, then ascended a snow-filled canyon to a pass lying between the headwaters of the Elwha and Queets. The men paused long enough to explore the divide, noting the bearings of peaks and the courses of rivers. Olympus stood in full view to the west, and the men concluded it was the source of several rivers that headed in the glaciers, then radiated outward in various directions. The men then descended to a basin at the head of the Queets and camped by Pluto's Gulch at the foot of Mount Olympus.

The march to Olympus had taken a week. Before attempting to scale the peak, the men decided to reconnoiter. Linsley and Fisher climbed along the south edge of a glacier until they reached a vantage point. They concluded, from their observations, that the southwest side of the mountain looked the most feasible to climb.

Linsley's party headed down the Queets to work around to the southwest side of Olympus, but, when the men were crossing rough terrain, Private Fisher became separated from his companions. Consequently, he traveled alone down the Queets to the ocean, where he was befriended by Indians, then walked the beach to Grays Harbor. Meanwhile, the Linsley party climbed the southeast side of Olympus to the head of a glacier, where they made a temporary high camp. From this point, Linsley, Bretherton, and Danton climbed what they took to be Olympus, and placed the copper box near the summit. So far as is presently known, the box remains unfound, but the evidence strongly suggests that the men climbed one of the peaks of Athena, the "South Peak" of Olympus.

Although the Olympus party was supposed to split up after the ascent, and travel down the Hoh and branches of the Quillayute, the men concluded that the sooner they reached civilization the better, because they were almost shoeless and their rations were running short. They therefore followed the Queets, which led directly to the ocean. Like Fisher, they were aided by the Indians, and they traveled down the beach to Grays Harbor.

During the absence of the Mount Olympus party, the pack train made a round trip to Hoodsport, returning with a load of provisions. Meanwhile, the men completed the trail to the point where the Hoquiam people had agreed to meet them. During this time they lost a mule which plunged over a cliff after being severely stung by yellow jackets.

On September 24, O'Neil divided the expedition's "Southern Division." He sent four men with the pack train to Vancouver Barracks via Quinault Lake and Grays Harbor. Accompanied by the remaining men, the lieutenant once again directed his

Placing the Oregon Alpine Club box and flag on the summit of "Mount Olympus" (Reproduced from Steel Points [July, 1907])

attention to exploration. Two settlers had more or less attached themselves to the expedition, and O'Neil now made use of their services. He dispatched a sergeant and one settler to investigate the Humptulips, while he, the two Churches, and the other settler set out to reconnoiter the Raft and Queets rivers.

O'Neil headed up the North Fork Quinault, but he left the stream after going several miles and climbed to the Queets-Quinault divide. At this point he dispatched the Churches to the Queets, while he and the other settler headed southward along the divide to explore the Raft; they missed the river, however, and wound up at Quinault Lake, then traveled with the Indians to the ocean in a dugout canoe.

The three exploring parties were reunited in Hoquiam, and on October 4 the town's inhabitants gave them a splendid banquet. The explorers then returned to Vancouver Barracks.

The Oregon Alpine Club was satisfied with its expedition but the cost had been higher than expected. On October 22, the club honored the explorers with another banquet, this one in Portland. Less than a month later, on November 16, 1890, O'Neil submitted his official report to the Assistant Adjutant General, Department of the Columbia.

The expedition had explored the southern half of the Olympic Peninsula. O'Neil wrote in some detail about the topography, the streams, and the resources, noting that timber would be the great product of the region for many years. However, much of the district was rough and precipitous, and O'Neil suggested that it be set aside as a national park.

On December 6, 1890, O'Neil gave a public lecture in

Members of The Mountaineers reenacting the placement of the copper box, 1973 (Photo by the author)

Portland. He concluded his presentation by again recommending that a national park be created. He lived to see his wish come true. The United States Congress created Olympic National Park on June 29, 1938, just four weeks prior to his death, but nearly half a century after he and James Wickersham made the first proposals for a park.

Lieutenant O'Neil, who became a brigadier general in World War I, did more than anyone else to lift the veil of mystery from the Olympics. His 1885 reconnaissance provided a preview of what the region was like; his larger 1890 expedition completed the task. The latter expedition built a pack trail across the almost impenetrable mountains, and this path became a major route of entry into the Olympics, one that is still used today.

O'Neil's 1890 expedition was one of the last "land expeditions." Together with his contemporaries—the Press Expedition, the Banner Party, the Gilmans, and others—O'Neil made the Olympics known. After 1890, the region could no longer be called *terra incognita*.

7

Advent of Mountaineering

THE EXPEDITIONS WHICH EXPLORED the Olympic Mountains in the latter part of the nineteenth century examined just about everything except the northwestern district; consequently, the hot springs—both Olympic and Sol Duc—were overlooked. These and other features of this last, northwestern quadrant gradually became known through, at first, reports of prospectors and hunters, and then later on by the Dodwell-Rixon survey party's detailed examination.

However, many years prior to the coming of Europeans to the peninsula, the Indians had visited the hot springs, and the tribal legends told of their origin. Once upon a time, two great dragons, Elwha and Sol Duc, engaged in mortal combat. Although they fought fiercely, neither could subdue the other. Each then took refuge in his lair, sealed the entrance, and wept from mortification. The dragons' hot tears were the "fire chuck," as the Indians called the hot springs.

Theodore Moritz, who lived in the Quillayute valley, befriended a wounded Indian in the 1880s. To repay Moritz for his kindness, the Indian took him to see Sol Duc Hot Springs. Moritz failed to respect the rights of the Indians to ownership; he filed a claim on the land and built a pack horse trail and a primitive spa.

Michael Earles acquired the hot springs after Moritz died in 1909, and built a resort which opened in 1912. The place was popular but short-lived, destroyed by fire four years later. The hotel was never rebuilt, but a store, swimming pool, and cabins were constructed.

Andrew Jacobsen discovered Olympic Hot Springs in September 1892, when returning from a hunting trip in a remote district southwest of Port Angeles. He did not linger to investigate the phenomenon because he thought the mountain was going to explode. When he mentioned what he had stumbled upon, people did not believe him, but fifteen years later William Everett "rediscovered" the hot springs while hunting cougar. Everett eventually acquired the land and developed the Olympic Hot Springs resort, a popular spa for many years.

Despite what had been learned by the pioneer expeditions, the Olympics remained mysterious. After the explorers left, the mountains attracted little attention for a decade or so, and visitors were few. Although "mountain men" had drifted through the Olympics since the 1850s, they were never numerous. But the expeditions opened the gates, and ever-increasing numbers of hunters, campers, mountaineers, and prospectors filtered into the rugged interior. This led to development of hotels and resorts on the shores of the larger lakes and at the hot springs.

Lieutenant O'Neil's trail up the North Fork Skokomish focused attention on the Lake Cushman area, and it became known as "the gateway to the Olympics," because Ida Finch called her Hoodsport hotel the Gateway Inn. O'Neil's second expedition was just starting when William T. Putnam and W. B. Lake opened Cushman House on the lake in July 1890. This was a restaurant housed in a tent on the eastern shore. The next year the men purchased three hundred acres on the west side, where they built a hotel and cottages. Two years later Putnam became sole owner of the business, which offered plain but comfortable accommodations. The adjacent farm produced almost everything served to the hotel's patrons.

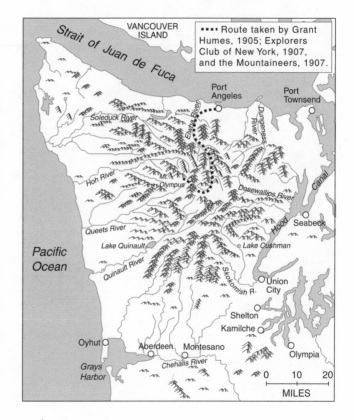

During the early 1890s, Russell Homan and Stanley Hopper built The Antlers. This log structure was also located on the west side, about a quarter mile south of Cushman House.

The resorts were built because the excellent hunting and fishing attracted people. The fishing was especially renowned, both in the lake and in the nearby river. The splendid scenery lured sightseers, and during the summer and fall mountain climbers left the hotels almost daily. A favorite ascent was Mount Ellinor, which overlooked the lake.

Russell Homan invited a friend, C.C. Maring, to accompany him on a pack trip in the Olympics in 1895. Maring traveled by steamer from Seattle to Hoodsport, then took the stage to Lake Cushman, where the party spent several days at The Antlers preparing for the trip. The group consisted of Russell Homan, Stanley Hopper, C.C. Maring, and two helpers, plus five pack horses and a dog. The little party left the lake on July 27, 1895. Although the men were tempted to linger along the way and fish the Skokomish, they moved steadily up the valley and camped the first night in the last of several log cabins built by settlers to hold down timber claims. Beyond this point (near the present-day Staircase Ranger Station), the men lost contact

John V. Finch and his family; his wife Ida ran the Gateway Inn
(Photo courtesy Robert V. Finch)

with civilization until they returned to the lake. Near the O'Neil expedition's seventh camp, the trail became less distinct, and the men saw the tracks of elk, deer, bear, wolf, and cougar, but not the animals themselves.

The party reached North Pass on the First Divide—the watershed between the Duckabush and Skokomish—late the second day. Because the views in every direction were magnificent, they named the place Camp Lookabout. Nearby were green meadows, with patches of snow bordered by wildflowers in bloom. Mount Steel soared above the camp, and the glacier on Mount Skokomish was "broken by several huge crevasses, and the peculiar greenish-blue color of the ice showed distinctly from beneath its covering of snow." The party remained at Camp Lookabout more than a week, making daily hikes in different directions. Hopper, the party's hunter, kept the table supplied with grouse, a welcome change from bacon, ham, and corned beef. During these side trips, the men did not see any large game, but signs of their presence were plentiful.

The little band moved on to the main divide, the watershed between streams flowing to the Pacific and to Hood Canal. Because one pack horse had been lost and another disabled, the men had to carry fifty-pound backpacks. When they reached the subalpine basin at the head of the Duckabush, they set up Elk Camp, pitching their tent near Marmot Lake.

The men made short exploring trips from Elk Camp, and on one of them shot an elk. "A snow drift near camp made a perfect refrigerator" in which to store the meat, and as a consequence they "feasted on elk steak" as long as they remained in the Olympics.

During the exploring jaunts, travel was made easier by the network of elk trails that crisscrossed the country. Maring summed up the men's impression of the mountains: "The Olympics are certainly a paradise for the artist, the hunter, the naturalist, and the explorer. They have only to become more generally known to be visited and appreciated. . . . This region is so full of nature's beauties that it might well rival the Yellowstone region as a national park."

Like Wickersham's and O'Neil's 1890 proposals, Maring's 1895 comment was prophetic, perhaps an indication of the growing recognition that the Olympics were outstanding, if not unique, and worthy of inclusion in a national park, the highest form of preservation provided by the United States government. In fact, the battle over the primeval Olympic forest really began when President Grover Cleveland created the Olympic Forest Reserve in 1897. This action culminated with the establishment, about forty years later, of Olympic National Park, but its immediate effect was withdrawal of more than two million acres on the Olympic Peninsula from settlement and entry. The reserve took in all the mountainous area plus extensive lowlands along the Pacific Coast, and most of this vast area was heavily timbered. The reserve was set aside to ensure the "preservation of its forest resources from wasteful destruction."

Henry Gannett, the United States Geological Survey's geographer, undertook a detailed survey of the new reserve. He employed two young men, each at $150 a month, to do the field work. Theodore F. Rixon was an engineer who had been a railroad surveyor but had shifted to timber cruising; Arthur Dodwell was a land surveyor employed by the government.

Accompanied by Gannett and two assistants, Dodwell and Rixon climbed Mount Ellinor on a lovely spring day in 1898 to look at the area to be surveyed. They gazed in awe at the snow-crowned peaks, the forest-choked valleys and canyons, and Gannett is reputed to have told them: "There's your work, boys. Go to it."

They did. Together with assistants, the men often worked sixteen to eighteen hours a day running compass lines, triangulating, checking altitudes with an aneroid barometer, photographing the country with a dry-plate camera, and recording the timber species and estimating the extent of the stands. They

The Antlers, a resort on Lake Cushman, early 1900s (Photo courtesy Robert V. Finch)

usually covered six to eight miles a day—a good showing in such rugged terrain. The survey lasted from 1898 through 1900. The men examined the lowlands and foothills during the winter and spring, then traveled through the high country in the summer and fall. Often, when operating at the higher altitudes, they climbed peaks that were not technically difficult—occasionally just for pleasure, but usually in order to do their work.

Their examinations were meticulous, with estimates made for each section of land as to: "the timbered, burned, cut, and non-timbered areas; the depth of humus and forest litter; the total stand of timber, and the stand of the principal species recognized by the lumber trade; the average height, diameter, and clear length, and the percentage of dead and diseased trees." The surveyors noted that the figures were estimates only, but pointed out they were based upon observations made by trained men.

The United States Geological Survey published the results in 1902. The survey had encompassed 3,483 square miles, or about half of the peninsula. Of this vast district, only 16 square miles had been logged at that time. The reserve contained 61 billion board feet of merchantable timber—"sufficient to supply the entire United States demand for two years."

Theodore F. Rixon, who together with Arthur Dodwell made the first survey of the Olympics, 1898–1900 (Photo courtesy National Park Service)

Arthur Dodwell (Photo courtesy National Park Service)

The report stated that, taken as a whole, the peninsula was "the most heavily forested region of Washington, and, with few exceptions, the most heavily forested region of the country." The densest forests were near the Pacific coast in the northwestern part and on the southern slope; while in the mountains, with increasing elevation, the forests became less dense and the species of less value for lumber.

The report included 750,000 acres that had been eliminated from the reserve at the turn of the century—reductions made due to pressure by timber interests, on the pretexts that the timber was not worth preserving, because it would be destroyed by storms, and that the land was good for farming. In reality, only a minuscule part of the deleted acreage was suitable for agriculture. Another argument for deletion was the contention that twenty miles of seacoast could be restored to use by eliminating it from the reserve. Ironically, a half-century later the United States Government had to purchase the eliminated coastland—which had been public domain in 1900—in order to include the beaches in Olympic National Park. Had the area been retained instead of deleted, the coastal strip could have been added to the park without cost to taxpayers.

Jack McGlone, a member of the survey team, made the first verified ascent of East Peak, one of several pinnacles that comprise the summit of Mount Olympus. His solo climb occurred in 1899, either in late August or early September. (The date is

usually given as August 12, but that was the probable date of the newspaper clipping found on the summit, so the ascent must have been some days later.) McGlone was filled with the spirit of adventure, and on more than one occasion he had climbed a peak "just to have a look around."

The surveyors had been encamped in Elwha Basin for about two weeks when Theodore Rixon and McGlone spent a day hiking merely for pleasure. They ascended the Elwha Snowfinger to the "Elwha Pass," then circled around the rim of Queets Basin to some rocks above Humes Glacier. Although night was quickly approaching, and Rixon was anxious to return to camp, McGlone impulsively decided to climb the big mountain. Before Rixon realized what was happening, McGlone had climbed down the rocks onto the glacier and was starting to make the ascent. Rixon shouted, suggesting that McGlone wait until the next day, when he or perhaps the entire party would go with him. McGlone may not have heard him; at any rate, he was already ascending the glacier and did not turn back. Rixon watched him until he disappeared from view near the glacier's head.

McGlone pressed on through the night, probably assisted by moonlight. Apparently, he reached the summit of East Peak

Mount Duckabush and Heart Lake in the Olympic high country (Photo by Frank O. Shaw)

several hours after sunset. This was the first ascent of one of the major peaks of Mount Olympus. The little Irishman left an unsigned scrap of newspaper in a tin can to record his feat, built a cairn over the can, then headed back toward Elwha Basin at two o'clock in the morning. The fragment of paper he left on the top lay undisturbed for eight years—until 1907, when several members of The Mountaineers climbed Olympus. The climbers found McGlone's newspaper record and they deduced, from items contained in the fragment, that it probably came from the *Mason County Journal*, dated either August 12 or 19, 1899.

The survey of the Olympics contains a bit of romance. In 1895, while working in the Lake Crescent district, Theodore Rixon met Caroline Jones, a single woman living alone at the western end of the lake. She was chopping wood when he approached and relieved her of her task. They became acquainted and were married later that year. He named Mount Carrie, the highest peak in the Bailey Range, in her honor.

The government's survey at the turn of the century marked the close of the exploration era in the Olympics, and the beginning of mountaineering *per se*. Mount Olympus was the prime attraction, not only because it was the highest mountain on the peninsula but also because, despite claims to the contrary, its highest pinnacle, West Peak, had never been climbed. Actually, not much was known about Mount Olympus in 1900. We know today that it is a massive, sprawling mountain with many crags, spurs, and pinnacles poking through and above a thick icecap. In fact, the area above timberline covers more than thirty square miles—almost an entire township—and the glaciers and icefields encompass about twelve square miles, making Olympus the third most glaciated peak in the United States, excluding the mountains in Alaska. The peak was an attractive goal, a plum waiting to be plucked. (An alleged ascent in 1854 is generally discredited by historians. The men Lieutenant O'Neil dispatched in 1890 climbed the southern flanks of the mountain, reaching the top of a lesser pinnacle, and McGlone, in 1899, was the first person atop East Peak. But West Peak, the highest of all, had not been scaled.)

The first serious attempt to climb Olympus in the twentieth century occurred in late August 1905, when Grant Humes set out with two companions to ascend "this little-known but much-talked of peak." His party traveled up the Elwha to the subalpine Elwha Basin, then ascended the Elwha Snowfinger to the Elwha-Queets divide. This was the elusive "Elwha Pass" which the Press Expedition sought but never found; it is known today as Dodwell-Rixon Pass. The route from the upper Elwha Basin was "strewn with slippery boulders of all sizes," which made travel difficult, and the Elwha, hemmed in by steep walls, "plunged and foamed" as it raced toward the valley below. The men had to cross the stream numerous times, "jumping from rock to rock or fording the icy torrent." Once they were on the Elwha Snowfinger, however, travel was easier, but still dangerous, because the snowfinger was undermined in the lower part with moulins, vertical well-like shafts in the ice that were up to fifteen feet in diameter, and "as round as if bored with a huge auger." Looking down into them, the climbers could see "the foaming, roaring torrent, rushing along with awe-inspiring fury."

At the pass the men had their first close view of Mount Olympus. The eastern slope was "for the most part occupied by the Queets glacier" (renamed Humes Glacier two years later), and from the glacier enormous blocks of ice broke loose at intervals and crashed into the canyon below. The men made camp in Queets Basin, where bears were feasting on huckleberries. The next morning they were "up with the sun" and headed for the summit, first climbing back to the main divide; they "proceeded westerly along the crest of a sharp rocky ridge" until they found a place where they could slide down snowfields to the Hoh Glacier. Huge chunks of ice were breaking loose from the foot of the glacier and tumbling into the newly born Hoh River, "making the mountains echo with the almost continual rumbling." By midday the summit appeared to be "scarcely a mile away, its triple crown glistening in the bright sunlight." However, the distance was somewhat greater than it looked. Up to this point the day had been ideal for climbing, but dense banks of fog now

moved in from the ocean side, threatening to engulf the party, and the men thought it prudent to retreat.

When they were returning to their previous night's camp, the climbers discovered a shortcut "by following the tracks of a bear in the snow through a narrow pass." This gap, subsequently known as Bear Pass, saved about two miles of rough going. Cold rain fell during the night, and because they were not prepared for severe weather, the men broke camp and left at daylight. They retraced their steps down the Elwha Snowfinger, then returned to Humes ranch via the Elwha trail.

Olympus slept again, but not for long. Fate intervened shortly afterward in the form of two mountaineering clubs that focused on the peak simultaneously. One of them, The Mountaineers, was new; the other, the Explorers Club of New York, was an old, established institution.

The formation of The Mountaineers came about as follows. On November 6, 1906, a volunteer committee, consisting of members of the Mazamas Club of Portland, Oregon, and other climbers living in Seattle, Washington, met to welcome Dr. Frederick Cook's party when it returned from an alleged successful ascent of Mount McKinley. This committee drafted a resolution calling for the appointment of another committee which would confer with the Mazamas and the Sierra Club in order to ascertain what form of local club could be established "to best promote the interests of the parent clubs." This committee was further directed to arrange for a meeting, at an early date, of Seattle residents interested in mountain climbing, to discuss the formation of a club.

Additional meetings were held later, and bylaws drafted and adopted, officers elected, and a permanent organization effected. The new club held its first meeting on January 18, 1907. The Mountaineers had 151 charter members, and it held its first local outing when members and their guests visited the West Point Lighthouse in Seattle.

The members decided to schedule an annual "summer outing," complete with packers and cooks, that would last from two to three weeks. The purpose of the outing was to climb, on each trip, one of the major peaks in Washington State. The Olympic Mountains were chosen to be the site of the first outing—to be held in the summer of 1907—with the object in view of making the initial ascent of Mount Olympus. This would be the first large party attempting to "conquer" Olympus, but the outing's organizers never suspected they would spark a race between two competing teams of alpinists. Thus was the stage set for a tug of war between The Mountaineers of Seattle and the Explorers Club of New York.

Several Explorers Club members recognized a rare opportunity when they were apprised of The Mountaineers' plan to make the first ascent of Mount Olympus during the club's 1907 outing. A trio from the New York club quickly organized an expedition and rushed in to climb Olympus before The Mountaineers

Herschel C. Parker, who led the party that made the first ascent of the Middle Peak of Mount Olympus (Photo courtesy The Explorers Club Archives, New York)

did. The elite climbers composing this little party were Herschel C. Parker, Professor of Physics at Columbia University; Walter G. Clark, an engineer; and Belmore H. Browne, artist and writer. The men were members of the American Geographical Society,

Mountain climbers descending steep snow to reach the Hoh Glacier (Photo by the author)

Washington, D.C., and of the Explorers Club, New York. Parker had also been one of the founders, in 1902, of the American Alpine Club, and he had made numerous ascents—of Mount Blanc and the Matterhorn in the Alps; of Shasta, Hood, and Rainier in the western United States; and six first ascents in the Canadian Rockies. He and Browne had been with Dr. Frederick Cook's expedition to Mount McKinley in 1906, and in 1912 they would attempt to climb that mountain again. The guides hired for the Olympic adventure were Will E. Humes, who lived on the lower Elwha, and DeWitt C. Sisson (according to Clark), or Henry Sisson (according to Browne) of Port Angeles.

The party left Port Angeles on July 9—Parker's fortieth birthday—with supplies for five weeks, and "full equipment for cutting a trail." Sisson was in charge of the pack train; Humes joined the party later—either at Geyser Valley (according to Browne) or Elwha Basin (according to Clark). Because trail builders sent out by Port Angeles citizens at the instance of The Mountaineers had preceded them, the Explorers Club party contributed to them the amount of money they had expected to spend on the work, "and joined forces with them to complete the trail." When it was finished, the party made its base camp in the Elwha Basin, close to the snow line.

Everyone then struck out for Olympus, by first climbing the Elwha Snowfinger. The snow was broken by crevasses and dotted with deep potholes, so they roped together for safety. They climbed to the gap in the divide between the Elwha and the Queets, and gave to it the name Dodwell-Rixon Pass because they believed, erroneously, that the surveyors were "the first to cross over the pass for scientific geographical work."

The men then descended into Queets Basin to below the snow line and established Cloud Camp. At times they had glimpses of the Pacific Ocean beyond the cloud cover lying over the land. After reconnoitering, they decided they were camping too far from Olympus, and therefore moved to a new location they called Camp Olympus. This site was close to the terminus of an icefield which they named Humes Glacier for one of their guides. Here they prepared for the climb. They would take with them canned pemmican, a nourishing mixture of beef, beef suet, sugar, and currants, melted and run together. They also had crackers, chocolate, raisins, and tea.

The men began the climb at an early hour the next morning, and they were soon plodding up Humes Glacier, which was broken by numerous fissures that they were compelled to jump. They ascended at a fair speed toward a pass at the glacier's head, and upon reaching it they could look down onto another, larger glacier that appeared to be the source of the Hoh River, whereas the Humes Glacier lay at the head of the Queets. The men named the gap Explorers Pass for their club, but shortly afterward The Mountaineers renamed it Blizzard Pass for a very good reason.

The glacier to the north and below the climbers "stretched in one vast snowfield up to the foot of Mount Olympus," and from the pass the men had their first truly unobstructed view of the mountain. They descended steep snow slopes to the glacier. Although it was badly broken by crevasses, they were able to work their way forward by jumping the crevasses at narrow places. Because they were roped together, they did not hesitate to jump. "The day was hot, and the bright sun on the snow burned through the previously acquired coat of tan, and produced blisters." After a long walk up the glacier, they reached a "ridge of exposed rock at the base of the final peak." Here they stopped to brew tea over an alcohol lamp, and the hot liquid "instilled new life for the final climb."

After a bit of steep snow and loose boulders, the men reached the top of the mountain, and the scene, they thought, surpassed the view from most peaks having a much greater altitude. Glaciers descended from every side, and hundreds of snow-clad peaks and snowfields were in view, reaching down into the forest-filled ravines. The men were so impressed, in fact, that they thought the Olympics were "surely entitled to be christened the Alps of America."

The climbers stood atop Middle Peak, second highest pinnacle of Mount Olympus. The date was Wednesday, July 17, 1907. They searched the summit rocks, but could find no trace of anyone having preceded them. They marked their visit by building a cairn, and they left an American flag, and a note with the date. They had scaled the peak in advance of The Mountaineers and won the race. Or so they thought. But their elation was tempered by a little doubt, and they expressed the thought that a pinnacle west of them might be slightly higher than the point upon which they stood. But they had run out of time; they could not go over and climb it.

The men from the Explorers Club gave names to a number of natural features in the Mount Olympus area—to nineteen of them, in fact—but only two of the names (Humes Glacier and Dodwell-Rixon Pass) have endured to this day and are still used. Most of the names they gave were replaced, later, by names suggested by other people. The climbers also prepared a map of the Mount Olympus district.

Once they had climbed the mountain, the men didn't linger. They descended to Queets Basin, broke camp, and quickly packed out over the trail. When they reached Port Angeles, they announced to the world that Mount Olympus had been climbed, and they saw to it that accounts of the "first ascent" were hastily published. The stories appeared in the newspapers just as The Mountaineers were beginning their own outing to Olympus, and therein lies a tale.

8

The Olympic Summer Outings

THE MOUNTAINEERS GREW RAPIDLY, AND within months the club's membership included people living in several states and Canada. The members represented "almost every trade and profession," but teaching predominated. Eleven members were on the faculty of the University of Washington.

The club was vitally interested, from its beginning, in the conservation of natural resources and preservation of the landscape. The constitution and bylaws stated that the club's object was to explore the mountains, forests, and watercourses of the Pacific Northwest, and to gather into permanent form the history and traditions of the region. The club was, as well, to preserve, by protective legislation or otherwise, the natural beauty of the land, and to make expeditions to fulfill its objectives.

Early in 1907 the club decided, as previously noted, that the ascent of Mount Olympus would be the goal of the first annual outing. The participants would follow the Elwha River to the center of the Olympics and establish a base camp at the stream's headwaters. This was the least known part of the Olympics because the region was virtually inaccessible. Most of the peaks—including the highest, the West Peak of Olympus—had not been climbed, and many were unnamed, their altitudes unknown.

The driving force behind the first outing was a quartet: Cora S. Eaton, L.A. Nelson, Asahel Curtis, and W. Montelius Price. Accompanied by Grant Humes, Curtis and Price reconnoitered the area in late May 1907. They noted that the trail would have to be improved because it was obstructed by windfalls and obliterated in many places, and the only paths that led to the upper Elwha were elk trails. Although the high country was still deeply buried beneath winter's snow, the men climbed Mount Noyes once and Mount Queets twice in order to view the country. They did not attempt to ascend Mount Olympus because they could not leave their pack horses for more than twelve hours, and the soft snow made it impossible to climb the

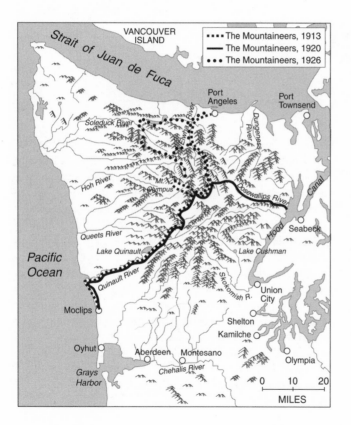

peak in that time. They noted the mountain was a great bulk clad with glaciers. This was remarkable because the peak rose only about eight thousand feet above sea level. The ascent did not appear to be difficult, and they thought that every member of the outing who wished to do so could climb the mountain.

The scouts could see that Olympus rose between the Hoh and Queets, therefore was isolated from the main range. In fact, its only connection with other peaks appeared to be the ridge extending eastward and forming the divide between the Queets, Hoh, and Elwha. The men decided the outing's temporary camp during the climb would be located on this east ridge.

The lack of a good trail into the area created a problem because the club did not have enough money to pay for building a path up the Elwha. However, the authorities in Port Angeles—and particularly banker W. R. Delabarre—were persuaded to come to the rescue. Delabarre succeeded in raising the necessary funds, and the town's residents turned out in force to do the work. They reopened the old Press Expedition trail into Press Valley and built a new one from the valley's head into Elwha Basin. This made it possible for everyone to reach Olympus and opened a permanent way into the region, "one of the most beautiful in the state."

Because the packers demanded prohibitive prices, the club purchased its own pack train, and employed Grant Humes to act as guide and packer. Enough provisions to last sixty-five or seventy people several weeks were then cached near the Elwha's headwaters, more than fifty miles from civilization.

The outing announcement noted that participants should understand that this was to be a camping trip, and that hotels where beds could be obtained would be left behind once the party entered the mountains. The outing was intended to be a pleasure trip with the participants relieved from packing supplies and cooking meals. The group would, therefore, provide a commissary outfit, the necessary provisions, stove, cooking utensils, general assembly tents, and enough tents to shelter the party. Also provided were the pack train and packers, cooks, and dishwashers. In addition, the pack train would carry up to fifty pounds of dunnage per person.

Each participant had to furnish personal effects such as sleeping bag or blankets, waterproof canvas or rubber poncho, suitable clothing, and miscellaneous items, including toiletries. The clothing included a "tramping suit" made of denim, khaki, or corduroy. Each woman was supposed to have one "durable waist" for tramping, another to wear around camp. "The skirt should be short," the regulations stated, "not much below the knee, and

Climber ascending Mount Meany during the summer 1907 outing (Photo by Henry Landes, reproduced from *The Mountaineer* 1, 3 [September 1907])

Members of The Mountaineers atop the West Peak of Mount Olympus on the occasion of the first ascent on August 13, 1907. Seated left to right: Anna Hubert, Charles E. Weaver, Henry Landes, Andrew W. Archer, and Earl E. Richards. Standing left to right: *Lorenz A. Nelson, W. Montelius Price, John B. Flett, Frank H. Plumb, and Charles Landes.* (Photo by Theodore C. Frye, Reproduced from *The Mountaineer* 1, 3 [September 1907])

under it should be worn bloomers." (The "Announcement of Final Plans for the Olympic Expedition," issued later, modified this slightly: "All women of the party who expect to go on side trips or climb any of the peaks must be prepared to wear bloomers or better still knickerbockers, as on all these trips no skirts will be allowed.") Underclothing, it was suggested, should be the kind one normally wore in winter. Everyone was supposed to have a broad-brimmed hat (to shield one from the hot sun), mosquito net, colored glasses (a "must" on glaciers), a haversack in which to carry lunch and water, and, finally, an alpenstock. Members who were musicians were encouraged to bring their instruments to provide campfire entertainment.

The cost to attend all three weeks of the outing was forty dollars per person.

With regard to planned activities, no one was required to climb Mount Olympus or any peak. In fact, if anyone proved to be not qualified to climb, he or she would be prohibited from doing so. At least one trip was scheduled each day, and often two, going to points of interest that could be visited in one day from base camp.

The Mountaineers were chagrined, but undaunted, shortly before the outing was scheduled to start, by newspaper stories telling about the "first ascent of Mount Olympus" by members of the Explorers Club of New York. They had rushed in and quietly made the ascent in advance of The Mountaineers, then hurried out and quickly published the details without giving credit to The Mountaineers, who had helped make the climb possible. Understandably, the latter, who had hoped to make the first ascent themselves, were nettled, and they found it particularly galling that the Explorers Club had stooped to this means to "steal" their peak.

The men from New York had hired Will Humes to guide them to Olympus, and Humes knew "where the way had been

"Greased up" members of the 1913 outing ready to climb (Photo by Mabel Furry, courtesy Special Collections, University of Washington Libraries, neg. no. 15272)

cleared" because he had previously served as a guide to The Mountaineers. Humes apparently did not realize the importance climbers attach to first ascents, and he also failed to recognize that a "conflict of interest" was present. Since the men from the Explorers Club had contributed money toward clearing the trail, and had also assisted in the work itself to some extent, and because the scheduled times of the two outings did not overlap, Humes apparently saw no reason not to accept the job. (But perhaps he should have understood, because his brother Grant was a member of The Mountaineers and one of the outing's participants.)

The sixty-four people on the outing were divided into two detachments, each group traveling by steamer from Seattle to Port Angeles. The first contingent, comprising three-fourths of the people, left as scheduled on July 24. The second group did not get under way until August 3. This detachment was largely composed of University of Washington faculty members whose duties prevented their leaving in July. At Port Angeles the men and women had a choice—they could either walk ten miles to the trailhead on the Elwha or ride the stage for a dollar. Because they were used to hiking, many elected to walk.

Among the participants were faculty members of three universities, nearly a score of other instructors, a few scientists, members of the legal and medical professions, a minister, and

representatives of various other professions and trades. In fact, the people came from all walks of life. However, dressed as they were in wilderness garb, everyone traveled "incognito," and this impression was heightened by the khaki suits which many wore and which almost gave "the appearance of a uniform." This "proved quite a disguise to rank." After traveling for several days through the primeval forest, one woman discovered by chance that a man in a "much-worn khaki suit" was a well-known writer whom she had long wished to meet; that another with a jolly laugh and ready wit was, when home in Seattle, "a most serious preacher of the gospel," and that a "smooth shaven young fellow with city looks and ways" was really a trapper who lived in the woods.

The hike up the Elwha took four days, and most of the way led through dense stands of conifers, alder, and vine maple. Near the end the trail quickly climbed into the subalpine forest zone, ending at the outing's base camp in a mountain meadow in Elwha Basin. The people traveled about ten miles a day. On the first day, they walked from Macdonald's Ranch to the Humes brothers' homestead in Geyser Valley. They encamped the next two nights at, respectively, Elkhorn Flat and Godkin Creek, then

Climbers in Marion Gorge on a tryout trip, 1913 outing
(Photo by R. L. Glisan, courtesy Special Collections, University of Washington Libraries, neg. no. 15202)

reached the base camp on the fourth day, which was a Sunday.

Elwha Basin was a lovely place, a beautiful upland meadow covered with grasses and wildflowers, and almost encircled by snow-clad peaks, the ones they were soon to climb. The area was doubly attractive because of its relative inaccessibility, lying as it did at the headwaters of the Elwha, Queets, and North Fork Quinault, almost forty miles from the nearest automobile road, and sixty miles from the closest railroad.

The outing was pleasant and enjoyable despite the fact that reveille always sounded at 4:30 A.M., if not earlier. The men and women roamed the high country daily, making "try out" or conditioning trips, followed by climbs of the various peaks. They saw deer, bear, grouse, and marmot almost every day, and now and then an elk. The hunting season was closed, but this did not diminish their pleasure in watching the wildlife. During the trek to and from base camp, many participants engaged in fishing the Elwha for trout. Several avid photographers were kept busy recording the sights and activities. The evening campfire was popular; here they entertained each other, sometimes with great hilarity. Official trips were not made on Sundays, but at least on one

Steep climbing near the summit of Mount Seattle, 1913 outing (Photo by P. M. McGregor, courtesy Special Collections, University of Washington Libraries, neg. no. 15263)

occasion two parties skipped the morning services in order to climb nearby peaks. However, they returned in time to attend the "most beautiful and impressive" evening campfire services, where they were surrounded by the "solemnity and majesty" of the snowy peaks, and "it was with a feeling of reverence that all finally wended their way silently to their beds beneath the stars."

The outing's activities were not, however, confined to daily walks and climbs, to views of glorious scenery, forests, and wild-life, to campsite festivities and religious rites. Never had climbers had "better or more elaborate meals" served them by smiling cooks who could create "delicious pies, cakes and other delicacies" without many of the most necessary ingredients. Using a small oven and a bonfire, the cooks baked bread every day, and served multi-course meals to from forty to seventy-five hungry climbers. Occasionally, the participants dined on fresh beefsteak which had been brought in "on the hoof" by driving livestock up the trail and butchering the animals in camp.

Mountain climbing was the principal activity, and it occupied most of each day. This was what they came for; consequently, they did not lose the opportunity to make several first ascents in

Climbers on the summit of Mount Seattle, 1913 outing
(Photo by Hec Abel, courtesy Special Collections, University of Washington Libraries, neg. no. 15264)

the heart of the Olympics. They would have made more, in fact, had not the Dodwell-Rixon surveyors climbed several peaks in the area less than a decade prior to their arrival.

During the outing, various numbers of climbers ascended ten peaks on twenty-one occasions. The number of climbers on each ascent ranged from a solo climb of a nearby peak to the forty-six who were on the first, unsuccessful attempt of Olympus. The largest successful climb consisted of forty-two people who topped Mount Noyes. When three climbers ascended East Peak—one of the pinnacles of Mount Olympus—on August 12, they discovered the unsigned scrap of paper left in a cairn by Jack McGlone in 1899 when he made his solo ascent from Queets Basin. The Mountaineers left the record of their ascent, and added: "We salute the brave pioneers who climbed in 1899."

The highlight of the outing, the "big climb" of Olympus, involved a two-day tramp and had been delayed until the latter part of the trip for two reasons: first, to give the participants experience in climbing lesser peaks; secondly, to await the arrival of the second detachment, so its members could participate. The trek to the mountain began on August 9, which "dawned gloomy and foggy," when forty-six excited Mountaineers left the Elwha Basin camp. Led by Asahel Curtis, they climbed, via Dodwell-Rixon Pass, to a temporary campsite in Queets Basin, "each individual, however slight, laden with his or her blankets and ten pounds of provisions." At the temporary camp the climbers made last-minute preparations, then retired in order to get an early start in the morning. When dawn broke on Saturday, August 10, clouds clung to the summits "and often rolled down into the valleys." This was an ominous sign, an indication the weather was deteriorating, but a little later the skies began to clear and several distant peaks came into view. The climbers "determined to make an attempt, at least, and if the storm broke away to push on to the summit." Everyone was cheerful and happy, despite "the poor prospect of success."

The mist had changed to rain, and a cold wind blew down the ice field by the time the climbers had gotten onto Humes Glacier, making the situation "anything but pleasant." Spurred onward by the cold, the climbers moved rapidly up the glacier, with the top of the mountain "now lost in the clouds." When they were about half-way up the glacier, "the rain changed to flurries of snow, swept along by a stiff wind."

Near the glacier's head the slope rose sharply, hiding the mountain beyond, and the climbers were somewhat protected from the storm. However, when they marched through the pass in the ridge, they were exposed to the full fury of the gale, and everyone's hopes sank. This was the gap that had been named Explorers Pass by the Explorers Club party on July 17, less than four weeks before, but The Mountaineers now gave it a more appropriate name: Blizzard Pass. Still, they continued to advance until the snowfield fell away to the Hoh Glacier at such a steep angle that its slope was invisible from the crest. The glacier, six hundred vertical feet below them, was hidden by storm clouds and a thirty-miles-per-hour gale was "whirling the snow along as it fell." The cliffs in the distance were lost to view and the party "appeared suspended in the heavens on the edge of some great cloud, with a white desolate world forming out of the chaos."

Because risking lives in such a storm was sheer folly just to reach a summit, the leaders decided to turn back. This was the only reasonable course to take. When the bugler sounded retreat, "a faint cheer went up," and almost immediately the "shivering group of people" made an about face, fell into line, and moved forward. They were, of course, disappointed, and an ordinary storm would not have prevented the ascent. But this "driving rain and snow storm"—which left a foot of fresh snow upon the upper levels of the mountain—was not an ordinary summer storm.

The most difficult task was still to come—getting a cold, half-exhausted party down the mountain safely. Once they started the descent, the climbers moved briskly along the glacier's edge, then onto the rocks, and it appeared as if everyone were out of danger. When they were just a half mile from the temporary camp, however, a small group became confused in the mist "and attempted to go down a steep draw to the snow-field." At this point Winona Bailey lost her footing "on the slippery, rain-soaked heather" and slid and tumbled over the rocks more than one hundred feet, "until she wedged under the snow at the base of the cliff." Miraculously, Bailey was not killed, but she did suffer severe injuries.

Dr. E. F. Stevens applied first aid, and a stretcher was hastily improvised from a rope wound around two alpenstocks. Bailey was then transported to the temporary camp. The climbing party now faced the difficult task of "fitting up a hospital in a driving rain, without even a tent for shelter, and caring for a helpless girl ten miles from the main camp, with that camp sixty miles in the heart of the mountains." However, they had no choice, and the doctor dressed Bailey's wounds under "the meager shelter afforded by a strip of canvas stretched against a rock."

Leaving a "hospital detail" to care for the injured climber until she could be moved, the balance of the party headed for the main camp in Elwha Basin. When the climbers approached Dodwell-Rixon Pass, they looked back and could see that fires had been built at Marmot Rock Hospital Camp—the name later given to the temporary campsite—"while to the westward the vast bulk

Mount Anderson from Sentinel Peak, 1920 outing (Photo by Mabel Furry, courtesy Special Collections, University of Washington Libraries, neg. no. 15268)

Poling the rapids of the Quinault River, 1920 outing (Photo by Elizabeth S. Lilly, courtesy Special Collections, University of Washington Libraries, neg. no. 15267)

of Mount Olympus shrouded in clouds refused even to bid them farewell."

The climbers reached base camp in Elwha Basin about sundown. The next day the "first comers"—those who had started out on July 24—began their four-day tramp down the Elwha. They left Port Angeles by steamer on August 14, just as twilight darkened into night. They were in Seattle at dawn on August 15, and for

them the first summer outing of The Mountaineers was over.

Meanwhile, the "hospital detail" remained in Queets Basin a week, attending the injured climber. On August 17, the little band transported her over the pass and down the Elwha Snowfinger to base camp.

On August 12, two days after the first climbers had been almost literally blown off Mount Olympus, ten men and one woman left Elwha Basin, determined to make the ascent. The party was led by Lorenz A. Nelson, and eight of the eleven had been on the August 10 climb that had been aborted. Obviously, they had not had enough of the mountain and were willing to challenge it again. Like the previous party, the climbers were hampered by stormy weather. The first day they traveled from Elwha Basin to Marmot Rock Hospital Camp, via Didwell-Rixon Pass. When crossing the pass, three climbers discovered a baking powder can lying on a knoll. The can contained a page from a magazine, upon which was written: "A.M. Godfrey, D.W. Starrett, W. Daggett, on our way to the Pacific from Port Townsend by Dungeness over Docewallups and Elwha Valleys,— Aug. 25, 1894." The Mountaineers added their own notation:

Fording the Quinault River, 1920 outing (Photo by Mabel Furry, courtesy Special Collections, University of Washington Libraries, neg. no. 15270)

"J.B. Flett, T.C. Frye, F.H. Plumb, three Mountaineers on their way to climb Mt. Olympus, Aug. 12, 1907." The men noticed that the trees in the pass and in Queets Basin bore old square blazes which they took to be the work of the 1894 party, because the blazes appeared to be about that old.

The next day Olympus was shrouded with clouds, and rain seemed likely. Undaunted, the climbing party left Hospital Camp before six a.m., and as the climbers ascended Humes Glacier the weather became colder and snow began to fall. This did not last long, however, "and the sun came out in all its splendor." The climbers zigzagged among the crevasses "that yawned on every side" until they reached Blizzard Pass. Here they had their first clear view of Olympus. The nearest pinnacle was East Peak, "with its clear-cut profile of a sphinx head"; to its left, and somewhat more distant, rose the "massive bulk" of Middle Peak, and still farther away stood West Peak, the highest point of all. (The fact that it was the highest was unknown at that time.)

Working their way down to the Hoh Glacier, the climbers lost six hundred feet of elevation, then began ascending the glacier. As the slope steepened, they took short rest breaks but kept "plugging away." Ignoring the lower East Peak, the climbers ascended

Mountaineer Helen Stout inspecting the marker identifying Camp Three of the 1920 outing (Photo by Frank O. Shaw)

Middle Peak, and upon reaching the top they found a cairn containing the record of the July 17 ascent by the Explorers Club. One of the New York climbers had added a comment to the effect that, while climbing, the men believed Middle Peak was the highest point, but after gaining its summit they were somewhat doubtful and thought perhaps the western pinnacle might be higher.

The view from Middle Peak surpassed expectations, and the climbers gazed in awe at the magnificent panorama. The Pacific Ocean was visible to the west, the Strait of Juan de Fuca and Vancouver Island to the north, and timbered ridges and foothills stretched endlessly to the south; but it was the view to the east that most captivated them: a splendid array of snow-clad peaks extending for miles, with Puget Sound visible through a gap. Beyond, in the far distance, were the great volcanic cones of the Cascades. Mount Hood, almost two hundred miles distant, was barely discernible to the southeast.

Now that they were so close, the climbers had no intention of letting West Peak escape, but they had no more than descended the western side of Middle Peak and moved out onto the glacial field, when the clouds closed down and obscured everything. Proceeding slowly, the climbers located what they took to be West Peak, but when the first three in line reached the top, "one of them gave a shout that died when half uttered," because at that precise moment the clouds parted, and perhaps a quarter mile

Preparing to start up the trail, 1926 outing (Photo courtesy Special Collections, University of Washington Libraries, neg. no. 15271)

distant rose their elusive goal. They had been deceived by the fog and had climbed Five Fingers Peak, a slightly lower mass of rock easily mistaken for West Peak when visibility is poor.

Quickly retracing their steps, they swung around to the north side of West Peak, and here they faced "real climbing." Led by Nelson, they slowly but steadily worked their way up to the summit. Upon reaching the top they searched thoroughly for

Trail along the High Divide (Photo by the author)

traces of former ascents but found nothing, and they concluded they were the first to set foot upon the highest point in the Olympic Mountains. The Mountaineers had won, after all, the little game of "first ascents" that climbers indulge in. "With a mighty cheer and then a song," Nelson wrote, "we started our task of cairn building, record writing, and picture taking."

The date was August 13, 1907, and the victorious alpinists were an illustrious group. Most were educators. Anna Hubert, the lone woman, taught in Seattle High School and was affiliated with Johns Hopkins University in Baltimore, Maryland; Charles E. Weaver was a University of California professor; Henry Landes and Theodore C. Frye were professors at the University of Washington; Frank H. Plumb was principal of Denny High School in Seattle; and Charles Landes and John B. Flett were Tacoma High School teachers. The others had varied occupations: Andrew W. Archer was proprietor of the Archer Linotyping Company; Earl E. Richards was a member of a freelance court reporting firm; W. Montelius Price was a salesman with the Seattle Electric Company; and the leader, Lorenz A. Nelson, a forester, worked for the United States Forest Service for years, and for two decades was head of the grading department of the West Coast Lumbermen's Association.

"The party left in the record box the following articles: United States flag, Mountaineers' badge, jack-knife, red and blue ribbon, purple string, ten cent piece, five cent piece, bread ticket, safety pin, a calk, hair pin, two matches and business card of A. W. Archer, containing account of The Mountaineers first attempt to climb Mount Olympus." Apparently, each climber wished to contribute something.

After descending West Peak, the climbers had to scale Middle Peak again in order to reach the Hoh Glacier, and they also had to climb six hundred feet to reach Blizzard Pass. However, twelve and a half hours after they had started out that morning, they were in Elwha Basin, where they found a warm dinner awaiting.

The rest of the summer outing was anticlimactic. Several days afterward, the remaining climbers packed their baggage, shouldered their knapsacks, and began hiking down the Elwha. A few days later the first summer outing of The Mountaineers was history. So, also, was the first ascent of Mount Olympus.

Less than a year later, on July 7, 1908, four Mountaineers from Bremerton, Washington—Henry H. Botten, George L. Hannaman, William Spaulding, and Alex Ormond—climbed the three main peaks of Olympus and returned to the Queets valley. This was the first time all three peaks were climbed in one day.

The club called The Mountaineers continued to grow, to increase its membership, and to explore the mountains, forests, and waterways of the Pacific Northwest. After its initial outing in the Olympics in 1907, the climbers turned their attention, during the next five summers, to the volcanoes of the Washington Cascades. The summer outings from 1908 through 1912 featured, in succession, Mount Baker, Mount Rainier, Glacier Peak, Mount Adams, and then Mount Rainier again. When 1913 rolled around, the alpinists once again headed to the Olympics for their seventh annual summer outing. The 1913 party was larger than the first one in 1907, having one hundred eight participants compared to sixty-four.

Earlier that year, Rudo L. Fromme, Supervisor of the Olympic National Forest, arranged for the Forest Service to build a new trail along the Queets-Quinault divide, in order that The Mountaineers could follow the ridge when leaving the Olympics via the Quinault. Fromme didn't find this an easy task to accomplish because then, as now, money for trail building and improvements was a scarce item in the Forest Service's budget. However, he did manage to get a small crew working up the North Fork Quinault—which had not been fully traversed by horses—to cut a way through windthrown trees and to scrape out switchback trails across deep canyons. Another crew was hurriedly cutting a trail along the divide. This made it possible for the outing to exit the Olympics via the Quinault.

The 1913 outing followed the same route in as The Mountaineers had taken in 1907—up the Elwha to its headwaters; but, instead of exiting via the same route as they entered, the party crossed the Low Divide, the central watershed, and followed the Quinault to the Pacific. This was the first large party and the first pack train to go across the mountains—or so The Mountaineers proclaimed. Perhaps they had never heard of the 1890 O'Neil expedition.

The summer outings of The Mountaineers were characterized by a traditional campfire program every evening, a feature the climbers looked forward to at the end of the day. With the entire party assembled around the fire, the group sang songs, performed skits, raised the flag above camp, and listened to serious lectures. Edmond S. Meany, a history professor at the University of Washington, was adept at lecturing. He was president of The Mountaineers from 1908 until his death in 1935, and he often recited the history and legends of the area the outing happened to be traversing. The 1913 outing was the first one held in the Olympics that Meany attended, and during the first night's campfire program he spoke about the history of the Olympics, relating Indian myths and legends. He told about the naming of peaks by George Davidson, the coast surveyor, and detailed the exploits of the Press Expedition, whose route they were following. As city editor of the *Seattle Press* in 1889, Meany had helped organize the expedition, and the explorers had named a mountain for him. Mount Meany was one of the peaks scheduled to be climbed during the outing.

Following the 1907 precedent, the 1913 outing traveled up the Elwha in stages, taking four days to reach base camp in Elwha

Basin. The original plan called for the camp to be located in Queets Basin, "the promised land"— in full view of Olympus, where the party would spend ten days in a beautiful natural park with scattered trees, rocks, brooks, and flowers. However, this plan proved to be impractical due to heavy snow, which made it impossible to take pack animals over Dodwell-Rixon Pass. Consequently, the leaders decided to use the site of the 1907 camp in Elwha Basin.

After a "try-out trip" and a climb of Mount Seattle, the alpinists turned their attention to Olympus. On August 11, sixty-seven Mountaineers climbed East Peak. Both the ascent and descent were "without incident, but not so the succeeding night in Queets Basin." Heavy rain fell, "and more than one conqueror of Olympus appeared half drowned at breakfast next morning," when the "mist and fog hung heavy and cold."

The new Forest Service trail, which had come about largely through the efforts of Supervisor Fromme, began at a junction with the North Fork Quinault Trail near Three Prune Creek and followed an old miners' path to a "flowery alpine meadow" on the divide. The trail then traversed south along the divide to Three Lakes and Finley Peak, beyond which it descended to the Quinault. This new path (first referred to as the Knife Edge Trail, much later as the Skyline Trail) had been "scarcely finished" before The Mountaineers began packing over it on August 20, on their way out of the Olympics. During the long trek down the new trail, the

climbers looked back time and again for a "last view" of Olympus, and then still "another last view of Mount Olympus."

One of the 1913 outing's highlights was floating in Indian dugout canoes, guided by Indians, down the Quinault River from Quinault Lake to the ocean. The boom of the surf announced the end of the journey, and The Mountaineers made their last camp on the ocean beach, gathered around the final campfire, heard the last stories, and stood with hands linked together while they sang the last good-night song. During the outing they had walked about seventy-five miles—not counting side trips to climb and explore—and had floated some thirty to thirty-five miles down the river. The next morning they hiked another nine miles down the beach to Moclips, where they boarded a train for Seattle.

In the spring of 1916, Mountaineer George E. Wright conferred with Forest Supervisor Fromme regarding trail work, and the parties "agreed that another Olympic outing should not be conducted until the so-called Promise Creek trail was in readiness, and, if possible, a trail from Elwha Basin to Dodwell-Rixon Pass." World War I delayed matters, but by 1920 the conditions were again favorable, and that summer The Mountaineers returned to the Olympics for their fourteenth annual summer outing, this time accompanied by Supervisor Fromme.

The 1920 outing differed from the two prior ones in that the 1907 and 1913 outings had both gone up the Elwha to the Elwha

Basin. The 1907 outing had returned via the same route, but the 1913 trip had exited via the Quinault, having thus crossed the Olympics from north to south. The plan for the 1920 outing was to approach the upper Elwha via the trail that led up the Dosewallips and down the Hayes, the former having been completed in 1915, the latter in 1917. This made it possible for the outing to have two main camps—one at the head of the Dose-wallips, another in Elwha Basin; but it also meant that the climbers would have access to more peaks than they would have time to ascend. However, having a second base camp in Elwha Basin would permit, as in 1907 and 1913, the climb of Mount Olympus and its satellites, the core peaks in the Olympic Mountains. The 1920 outing would come out of the mountains via the North Fork Quinault and—by utilizing the new Promise Creek Trail—the divide between the Queets and Quinault. As in 1913, the participants were scheduled to float down the Quinault River from Quinault Lake to the ocean in Indian dug-out canoes, then hike the beach to Moclips.

Except for one day, the 1920 outing was blessed with three weeks of continuous sunshine, which was a novelty on outings in the Olympics that lasted more than a few days. The people spent five days at the main camp at the head of the Dosewallips, and they voted this camp to be the most attractive one, located as it was in the subalpine meadows on a terrace below Hayden Pass.

The most prominent peak in this district was Mount Anderson, "its broad flank glacier-clad, double summitted, sharply cutting the sky with broken toothed edge." And, far to the west, "rose the vast bulk of Olympus" and the peaks encircling Elwha Basin.

Mount Anderson was the lodestone that attracted the most attention. The opportunity to make the first ascent of a major peak did not occur often on the summer outings of The Mountaineers; however, "the most notable single accomplishment of the 1920 outing was the successful climb of Mount Anderson." After a couple of scouting trips, a party of thirteen led by Fairman Lee climbed the peak on August 5.

The outing then moved its base camp to Elwha Basin, and on August 10 fifty climbers set out for Olympus, following the footsteps of their predecessors. The climb itself was uneventful. While encamped in the basin, the climbers ascended four of the "Elwha Basin peaks." The days raced by, as they always did on the summer outings. On August 14 the men and women broke camp in Elwha Basin, traveled down the North Fork Quinault as far as Promise Creek, then took the mile-high Queets-Quinault divide and eventually dropped to Quinault Lake. Here they parted company with their pack train, and, like the participants in the 1913 outing, they stepped into canoes with Indian guides and floated down the Quinault River to the ocean, where they made their last camp on the beach.

From 1921 through 1925, The Mountaineers held their outings in the Washington Cascades, and also at Mount Garibaldi in British Columbia and Glacier National Park in Montana. By the time 1926 rolled around, it had been six years since the participants of the summer outing had trod the Olympic trails. So once again the climbers headed for the mountains west of Puget Sound. This was the club's twentieth annual summer outing. The party, made up of 104 climbers, took a night steamer to Port Angeles, then traveled by stage west of the town. They crossed their old friend, the Elwha, hastened onward past Lake Crescent, then followed the Soleduck River to the hot springs. After considering other possible routes of entry, the outing committee had decided the climbers would visit the northwestern corner of the Olympics, the least explored area on the Olympic Peninsula. This would also permit those climbers who had not yet ascended Olympus to climb the peak, thus chipping one more notch in their alpenstocks.

The outing traveled from the hot springs to Deer Lake and Seven Lakes Basin, and on to Soleduck Park at the river's headwaters. The weather was not good—the party hiked through typical Olympic drizzle at first; then, much to everyone's dismay, the views were obscured because the country was "alternately hidden by fog and swept with fine rain." The permanent camp was set up on the High Divide.

Pack horses at Deer Lake (Photo by the author)

This was the first time the club had attempted to climb Olympus from the north, but seventy-one climbers made the strenuous trek, which called for descending four thousand feet from the High Divide to the Hoh River, then climbing seven thousand feet to the mountain's summit. The climbers moved up the Blue Glacier, with the mountain walls obscured by swirling clouds and fog banks. Nevertheless, after numerous delays, when the scouts ahead were "trying to find the mountain," the climbers ascended Middle Peak—the largest party ever to scale the pinnacle. The climbers then descended to Olympus Camp, in the meadow country just below Blue Glacier, and the next day hiked down to the Hoh River, then made the strenuous climb back up to the High Divide.

The outing now moved to Appleton Park, on the divide between the Soleduck and the Elwha. Two days later it moved again, the route leading past Olympic Hot Springs, then along Boulder Creek and the Elwha River to the Elwha Ranger Station. Here the camp was expanded by the second-weekers who had arrived, and that evening's campfire was the largest yet, with 116 Mountaineers and numerous visitors creating a large, fire-lit circle. "This was the last memorable feature of the Outing for some members, the first impression of what was to come for others." The next day the adventurers began the long trek up the Elwha River to Elwha Basin.

Each outing The Mountaineers held in the Olympics had been located, at one time or another, in Elwha Basin. The first-weekers having climbed Olympus from the north, the second-weekers now set out to ascend the peak via the old southeastern route. They did not waste time. They had no more than arrived in the basin than twenty-two ambitious climbers left the next morning, intent on scaling East Peak. They ran into difficult going, and noted that, due to light snowfall the preceding winter, the Elwha Snowfinger had shrunk and had greatly changed in appearance. Beginning the ascent from Hospital Camp in Queets Basin, the climbers were quickly forced to retreat "due to severe ice conditions," and had to abandon the climb.

On the way to ascend Olympus, the climbers had been accompanied as far as Dodwell-Rixon Pass by an "exploring group." Leaving the climbing party at the pass, the smaller band scrambled to the top of "a gentle little peak commanding a superb view," and christened the vantage point Winona Peak in honor of Winona Bailey, "the only person to have taken part in each of the four Olympic Summer Outings." The name was not destined to last, however, and the peak is known today as Bear Mountain, because of its proximity to Bear Pass.

After climbing several peaks, The Mountaineers moved from Elwha Basin to Low Divide, where members of the Olympic Chalet Company extended a hearty welcome. During the evening campfire program, F.W. Mathias told them about the company's plans to improve the trails and build shelter huts.

Breaking camp at Low Divide, the outing traveled to Quinault

Lake in "two long tramps." Then, following precedent, the members floated in Indian canoes from the lake to the ocean. But some Mountaineers noted a difference from the way it had been in 1913 and 1920. Now, in the quiet stretches, the bordering forests echoed with the sound of outboard motors, which contrasted strangely with memories, from the earlier outings, of the steady dip, dip, dip of paddles in the silent depths of green water.

The Mountaineers held their final campfire on the beach, with the black walls of trees behind them and the rolling combers stretching in phosphorescent lines at their feet. The next morning they walked the beach to Moclips, where they boarded the buses that would take them to Seattle. Like its predecessors, the 1926 summer outing had become part of the silent past.

During the years that followed, The Mountaineers held further summer outings in the Olympics, but the days of pioneering, of making new discoveries, were largely over—although for the participants themselves, individually, tramping through the mountains would ever be a new and fresh experience.

Mount Olympus from the Skyline Trail (Photo by Frank O. Shaw)

Terra Incognita *to National Park*

THE ERA OF EXPLORATION AND PIONEER climbing in the Olympic Mountains can be said to have ended with completion of the Olympic Highway on the peninsula in 1931. Now one could drive all the way around the mountains. The highway brought to an end the long years of isolation and inaccessibility.

The explorers and early climbers dispelled mysteries and discredited rumors about the Olympics. The mountains did not enclose a great central valley, a plateau of rolling prairies, or a huge lake having a subterranean outlet. Contrary to popular belief, deposits of valuable minerals were lacking. No fierce, cannibalistic Indians guarded the mythical paradise of rich lands awaiting settlement. The rivers originated in the mountain center, not on the outer slopes, as had been supposed. The most important discovery, perhaps, was the fact that the Olympics are not a range, but a jumbled cluster of peaks and ridges and canyons.

Until the explorers made their discoveries by on-the-scene investigations, the mountains had been *terra incognita*, the unknown land—except, possibly, to a few adventurous Indians. The Gilmans, the Press Party explorers, and the men on the second O'Neil expedition prepared maps depicting the country's configuration, the courses of rivers and minor streams, the locations of the higher peaks. The men photographed the country and named geographic features, thus adding to the nomenclature. The chief aspects of the Olympics were now revealed, and photographs would assist travelers in the interior to recognize "notable mountains and landmarks." Nevertheless, despite the fact that the explorers had dispelled widespread ignorance about what the interior was like, an aura of mystery lingered on for decades afterward.

Because they were human, the explorers made mistakes and at times reached erroneous conclusions. One must remember, however, that today the topography is known and the region is crisscrossed by trails. This was not the case a century ago. The maps at that time showed the peninsula's coastline reasonably well, but they were blank insofar as the interior was concerned. The men who accepted the challenge did not hesitate to enter an untouched, unknown wilderness and flag the way for future travelers.

One wonders at times just how much impact the explorers had upon later developments. This question is difficult to answer. The paths the explorers took often became the routes of the arterial trails that beckon today's backpackers to investigate the Olympics. One cannot say, however, that the expeditions "opened up" the country, because much of the region was too rough to attract settlers. Most of the peninsula's residents lived on lowlands bordering the mountains, not in the rugged interior. Moreover, the explorers' routes usually were the natural ones determined by the topography—the paths that most adventurers would have followed in any event.

Perhaps the most important contribution made by the explorers and pioneer climbers was the recognition, at an early date, that the Olympics were unique and of national park caliber. They set in motion the movement that culminated, about a

Old ranger station at Dosewallips Meadows (Photo by Frank O. Shaw)

Makeshift shelter cabin on the Upper Soleduck River (Photo by Frank O. Shaw)

of the Olympics since then can be stated succinctly: Exploitation versus Preservation.

Wickersham's and O'Neil's proposals were merely recommendations, and nothing was done at that time. The issue simmered, however, with the opening octaves of the "war" for the land sounding less than a decade later when President Grover Cleveland, by executive order, created the Olympic Forest Reserve in 1897. This action withdrew from settlement and entry about one-half of the peninsula. Shortly afterward the government surveyed the reserve, at the same time significantly reducing its size due to pressure from the timber industry.

The reserve became the Olympic National Forest in 1905. Although creation of the reserve, or national forest, was a step toward conservation, it did not assure permanent protection of the ecosystem; it merely meant that, for better or worse, exploitation would be controlled. At best, it would delay by a few decades destruction of the primeval forest. Because they realized better protection was needed, various groups urged creation of a national park or a game refuge in the Olympics, in order to ensure that future generations could experience *de facto* wilderness, and also to save the elk herds that were being decimated by hunters who sold the animals' teeth for ornaments and souvenirs.

William E. Humphrey introduced legislation in Congress in 1906 and 1908 to create a "national game preserve" in the Olympics, "not only to preserve the game, but as a step toward a

half-century later, in the creation of Olympic National Park. The first proposals to give the Olympics national park status, made in 1890 by James Wickersham and Joseph P. O'Neil, were the signal, the flashing beacon light. The controversial history national park." President Theodore Roosevelt favored the bill, but it met strenuous opposition in Congress, failing to be approved in the Senate. Because it was impossible, before Roosevelt left office, to reintroduce and pass the bill, Humphrey convinced Roosevelt to proclaim the heart of the Olympics the Mount Olympus National Monument. This was done by executive order on March 2, 1909, under the authority of the Act for the Preservation of American Antiquities. This law, enacted in 1906, granted the president the power to establish national monuments by proclamation.

The monument contained 620,000 acres, or slightly less than one thousand square miles, but a large percentage of it was sub-alpine country. The balance was virgin forest having commercial as well as scenic value. The chief reason for establishing the monument was preservation of the elk herds, but it also protected the forest. However, within a few years timber interests succeeded in getting heavily forested lands deleted from the monument on three occasions. The largest reduction, during World War I, purportedly was made in order that prospectors might locate manganese ore deposits, a strategic metal needed in the armament program, but this was merely a ruse. No minerals were mined in

Grove of large spruce trees near the Olympus Ranger Station, about 1936 (Photo by George A. Grant, courtesy National Park Service)

Hoh Lake Shelter shrouded in fog in mid-August (Photo by the author)

the deleted area, which included the most heavily forested part of the monument. This reduction cut the monument's size from 620,000 acres to 328,000. Of the remaining acreage, fully three-quarters consisted of rugged country lying above the timberline or supporting noncommercial subalpine stands. Very little of the magnificent low-elevation, old-growth forest for which the Olympics were famed remained within the monument's new boundaries.

The monument was closed to trapping and hunting in 1927 to conserve the wildlife, and in 1933 its jurisdiction was transferred from the Forest Service to the National Park Service. Establishment of the national monument had suppressed, temporarily, the push for a national park. However, the monument was too small, especially after the land withdrawals, and monuments could be abolished or reduced in size by presidential proclamation without the concurrence of Congress.

As the years went by, the number of people visiting the Olympics steadily increased, and gradually the public became aware of the need to preserve the mountains in their natural state. Simultaneously, logging accelerated, with the old-growth forests visibly disappearing at an alarming rate. During the 1920s, the Grays Harbor mills alone cut almost one billion board feet each year, and most of that cutting was on the peninsula. Bleak, ugly, burned-over stumplands took the place of standing, living trees as the loggers cut and slashed their way ever closer to the foothills and the still inviolate snow-clad peaks.

The national park movement was revived in the 1930s, after completion of the Olympic Highway, which made the country more accessible, and this, in turn, brought increasing numbers of visitors to the mountains. Many people supported a park, and conservationists began a drive which culminated, in the mid-1930s, in the introduction of bills in Congress to establish an Olympic National Park. The park would be created by using the existing national monument as its core, then adding additional lands from the surrounding national forest. This plan did not sit well with the Forest Service, and in 1936, in an effort to defeat the park bills, it established the Olympic Primitive Area adjacent to the national monument. The primitive area was a farce; it consisted of several blocks of "high country" and included virtually no lowland forest. Essentially, it was a series of ridge-top projections that extended outward from the monument like the arms of an octopus. Moreover, the primitive area could be reduced in size or abolished at any time by the Secretary of Agriculture, under whose aegis it was established. On the other hand, a national park could be altered only by act of Congress.

President Franklin D. Roosevelt visited the Olympic Peninsula in 1937 and conferred with politicians, newspapermen, scientists, and officers of the National Park Service and the Forest Service. He favored a large park, and his visit gave impetus to the park movement. Eventually, after much debate pro and con, Congress created Olympic National Park on June 29, 1938.

The new park contained 648,000 acres of primitive land, all but 2,300 acres of it already owned by the federal government.

Within its boundaries were included all of the existing national monument, much of the Olympic Primitive Area, and other lands taken from the Olympic National Forest. The park was located mainly in the central and western Olympics; regrettably, it did not include most of the high peaks of the eastern Olympics, the ones visible from Puget Sound.

The law creating the park provided that the president could add, by proclamation, up to 250,292 acres. On several occasions the park was enlarged. The additions consisted of a large area of rough, mountainous country in the north and southeast, plus extensions down the western river valleys to include the best of the "rain forests," representative samples of the original forests of the Pacific Northwest. The additions also included the winter range of the elk herds, land fronting the Pacific Ocean for fifty miles, and a corridor along the Queets River. The last additions were made by President Harry S. Truman before he left office in 1953. These additions preserved the beaches, as well as one river all the way from the mountains to the sea.

The park was dedicated on June 15, 1946. In recent years, minor boundary adjustments have been made to facilitate administration, and presently the park contains about 900,000 acres. Excluding the coastal strip and river corridor, the park extends roughly forty miles from north to south, a like distance from east to west, and most of it remains in its natural state.

The Olympics today are not the wilderness that the explorers and first climbers encountered. The trackless forests that then stretched from the beaches to the high mountains are mostly gone. Today's visitors will find development, especially on lowlands surrounding the mountains: farms, stump ranches, cities and towns, and sawmills; roads and highways; and vast stretches of cutover land, in part supporting second-growth forest, but with much land not reforested. As far as the forests go, the grandeur of the past is mostly gone. And the mountains are not as wild as they once were. Almost every peak has been climbed, every ridge traversed, every canyon explored. About half the mountainous district—the half comprising the Olympics' rugged core—lies within the park. Here the country is still wild and primitive, little changed from how it looked when the first explorers traveled through the region.

Although the Olympic Mountains are now well known, visitors can still capture, to a limited extent, the mystery long associated with them. One has merely to leave the well-traveled trails and pack into the remote interior to roam through unchanged forest aisles, to tramp along fog-shrouded ridges. Then, lost in the magical enchantment wrought by the surroundings, one may walk silently in the footsteps of the pioneer explorers, the occasional daring Indian, and the "mountain men" who were the first to gaze upon this pristine wilderness.

Noted climber Glen Kelsey ascending steep snow near the summit of Mount Olympus, 1959 (Photo by the author)

Sources Cited

Listed below are the sources for the quotes that appear in this book, keyed by page.

Chapter 1

10   The statement that "The Indians are not known to have ever crossed the wild Olympic Mountains . . . " is from Eldridge Morse, "Notes on the History and Resources of Washington Territory, furnished Hubert Howe Bancroft of San Francisco, California, Volume 19," Bancroft Library, University of California, Berkeley.

13   The reference to the "land of snow and ice" is from Edmond S. Meany, "Indians of the Olympic Peninsula," *The Mountaineer* 13, 1 (November 1920), p. 34.

14   The quotations concerning Perez are from Hubert Howe Bancroft, *History of the Northwest Coast, Volume I, 1543–1800,* volume 27 of *The Works of Hubert Howe Bancroft* (San Francisco: A. L. Bancroft & Company, 1886), p. 157.

14   The assertion that Heceta and his crew were the first Europeans to set foot "on the soil of the Northwest Coast" is from Bancroft, *History of the Northwest Coast, Volume I,* p. 160.

14   Captain Cook's reference to "the pretended Strait of Juan de Fuca" is from Bancroft, *History of the Northwest Coast, Volume I,* p. 170.

18   The phrase "Oregon country" is from Gordon Speck, *Northwest Explorations* (Portland: Binford & Mort, 1954), p. 370.

18   The characterization of the treaty between the United States and England as one of "joint occupation" can be found in both Speck, *Northwest Explorations,* p. 370, and in Bancroft, *History of the Northwest Coast, Volume II, 1800–1846,* volume 27 of *The Works of Hubert Howe Bancroft* (San Francisco: The History Company, 1886), p. 338.

23   The "facts" regarding the alleged first ascent of Mount Olympus in 1854 were first published in George H. Himes, "First Ascent of Mount Olympus," *Steel Points* (Portland) 1, 4 (July 1907), p. 159.

Chapter 2

24   The description of the Watkinson Expedition can be found in Morse, "Notes on the History and Resources of Washington Territory."

27   The reference to Post Order 47 is taken from the return from Fort Townsend, Washington Territory for the

month of June 1882, "Returns from United States Military Posts 1800–1916," Microcopy 617, Roll 1284, National Archives, Washington, D.C.

27　Colonel Chambers' exploration of the mountains "in compliance with verbal instructions . . . " is cited in the Fort Townsend returns for the months of August and September 1882, "Returns from United States Military Posts 1800–1916."

29　The quotation "surveying the trail to Snowy Range" is taken from the return from the 21st Infantry for the month of May 1884, "Returns from Regular Army Infantry Regiments, 1821–1916," Microcopy 665, Roll 221, National Archives, Washington, D. C.

29　O'Neil's reference to his "youthful enthusiasm" is taken from his unpublished lecture notes, set no. 2, p. 2, Robert B. Hitchman Collection, Washington State Historical Society, Tacoma.

29　O'Neil's description of the "boldness and abruptness" of the Olympics as being an "impenetrable barrier . . . " is from his handwritten manuscript (with revisions) detailing his 1885 exploration, Robert B. Hitchman Collection, Washington State Historical Society, Tacoma.

30　The statement about General Nelson A. Miles's discrediting of the "wonderful stories" about the mountains and his surprise that "so much seemingly valuable territory should be unknown" is from O'Neil's handwritten manuscript.

31–41　Unless otherwise noted below, the quotations in the description of O'Neil's 1885 expedition are taken from his handwritten manuscript.

34　O'Neil's discovery that "the first good view of the Olympics . . . " was from the Sister Peaks is mentioned in his unpublished lecture notes, set. no. 2, pp. 20–21.

36　The quotations about the party's finding it "pleasant when traveling . . . "

to hear the marmots' cheerful call, and their "expenditure of much time, energy, and language" to rescue several mules are from O'Neil's unpublished lecture notes, set no. 2, pp. 17 and 20.

39　The statement referring to the source of the Elwha "and the field of ice from which it started" is from the edited version of O'Neil's handwritten manuscript, published by the *Seattle Press* on July 16, 1890, under the heading "O'Neil's Exploration—Record of his trip back of Port Angeles in 1885."

41　The quotation beginning "The country remained a *terra incognita* until 1885 . . . " is from O'Neil's unpublished lecture notes, set no. 4, pp. 2–3.

41　The quotation with reference to Noplace, "in the heart of the mountains," is from Joseph P. O'Neil, "Official Report to the Adjutant General on his Exploration of the Olympic Mountains," U. S. Senate, Document No. 59, 54th Congress, p. 19.

Chapter 3

42–47   The quotations describing the Gilmans' interest in and exploration of the Olympics are from S. C. Gilman, "Unknown No Longer," *Seattle Post-Intelligencer,* June 5, 1890.

47   The Gilmans' efforts to map out "a possible route for a railroad" are cited in Lucile H. Cleland, *Trails and Trials of the Pioneers of the Olympic Peninsula* (Humptulips Pioneer Association, 1959; facsimile reproduction, Seattle: Shorey Book Store, 1973), p. 255.

47   John J. Banta and S. Price Sharp's scouting "in search of a homestead . . . " is cited in Cleland, *Trails and Trials,* p. 255.

48–55   The quotations in the description of the Gilmans' December 1889 explorations are from John J. Banta's diary, "Memorandum of our exploring trip from Tacoma around the Straits of Juan de Fuca to Pysht Bay, and through the country south to Grays Harbor (S. P. Sharp, J. J. Banta), Dec. 3rd 1889 to Jan. 7th 1890," collection of Lelia Barney.

55   The characterization of the Gilmans' efforts as a "daring trip through the Olympic Peninsula in winter" that "led to the colonization of the Queets and Clearwater valleys" is from Cleland, *Trails and Trials,* p. 255.

55   The report that the Gilmans began "making arrangements to organize a colony" is from Banta, "Memorandum."

55   The term "Evergreen on the Queets" is from Gordon D. and Rowena L. Alcorn, "Evergreen on the Queets," *Oregon Historical Quarterly* 74, 1 (March 1973).

Chapter 4

56   Governor Ferry's statement that the Olympics were unknown "like the interior of Africa" was originally published in the *Seattle Evening Press,* October 23, 1889, and quoted in "The Olympics," *Seattle Press,* July 16, 1890, p. 1.

56   Christie's letter to the editor of the *Seattle Press,* in which he used the phrase "beyond the limits of civilization," was quoted in the paper's July 16, 1890 issue, p. 1.

56–76   Unless otherwise noted below, quotations in the description of the Press Expedition are drawn from a series of articles published by the *Seattle Press* on July 16, 1890 (see Selected Bibliography).

76   The description of the explorers' arrival at Aberdeen is from the *Aberdeen Bulletin,* as quoted in "The Olympic Range," *Portland Oregonian,* June 3, 1890.

Chapter 5

77–84   Unless otherwise noted below, the quotations in the description of Wickersham's first journey are from his handwritten notebook, "Sketches, A

Trip to the Olympic Mountains," transcribed by George Marshall. Copy of typescript, George Marshall Manuscript Group, Manuscript Section, University of Washington Libraries.

80   The description of the party as following elk trails "through a dense forest . . . " is from Charles W. Joynt, "The Unknown Olympics," *Mason County Journal,* May 23, 1890 (apparently reprinted from the *Buckley Banner*).

83   The statement that "the oft-repeated legend of the Indians was not altogether a myth" is from Joynt, "The Unknown Olympics."

84   The description of the route as passing "through the heart of the Olympics," the identification of one member of the Banner Party as "an old mineral prospector," and the comment that the party would "take up a line of march . . . " are from an article originally published in the *Buckley Banner* and

reprinted as "Belittling Lieut. O'Neil," *Seattle Press,* July 16, 1890.

85–86   Quotations in the description of the early stages of the Banner expedition (up to their arrival at O'Neil's Camp Five) are from "Olympic Mountains: Explorations Made by the Wickersham Party," unidentified newspaper story, Wickersham Papers, Manuscript Collection, University of Washington Libraries.

86–89   The quotations in the description of the Banner Party's encounter with the soldiers at Camp Five, ending with their doing "justice to the menu" are from H. Fisher [James B. Hanmore], "Lt. O'Neil's Exploration of the Olympic Mountains," handwritten manuscript, Mazamas' library, Portland, Oregon.

89   The statement that the women of the Banner Party "fulfilled their promise to Lieutenant O'Neil" is from B. J. Bretherton, "Olympic Adventure," *Tacoma Sunday Ledger,* August 17, 1890, p. 9.

89   The placement of the flag "upon a pinnacle of snow" is described in B. J. Bretherton, "Across the Divide," *Seattle Post-Intelligencer,* August 14, 1890, p. 9.

89   The statement that O'Neil left the flag in place as "a monument to the pluck and bravery . . . of the first ladies to cross the Olympic range" is from B. J. Bretherton, "Olympic Adventure."

89–93   Unless otherwise noted below, the quotations in the description of the Banner Party expedition from the time the explorers reached "the height of land in the central plateau" until they emerged at Hood Canal, having often "slept above clouds" are from James Wickersham, "A National Park in the Olympics . . . 1890," *The Living Wilderness* 77 (Summer-Fall 1961), pp. 6–11.

89   The inscription the Banner party carved on a tree, listing the names of those who reached Soldier Camp, is from B. J. Bretherton, "On the Duckabush," *Seattle Post-Intelligencer,* September 3, 1890.

90   The statement that Lake of the Holy Cross was so named because "the trunk of a once large tree . . . " with limbs that formed a cross was reflected in its waters is from Fisher, "Lt. O'Neil's Exploration."

93   Wickersham's description of the clothing worn by the women of the Banner Party is from "Olympic Mountains: Explorations Made by the Wickersham Party."

94–95   The quotations from Wickersham's letters on behalf of "a proposed Olympic National Park" can be found in Wickersham, "A National Park in the Olympics . . . 1890."

Chapter 6

98   The statement about "procuring one or two good shots" is from O'Neil's unpublished lecture notes, set no. 4, pp. 4–5.

99   The phrase "men, mules, and merchandise" is from Louis F.

Henderson, "Flora of the Olympics," *Steel Points* (Portland) 1, 4 (July 1907).

104   The naming of Jumbo's Leap "in honor of his [the dog's] daring skill as a mountaineer" is recorded in Fisher, "Lt. O'Neil's Exploration of the Olympic Mountains."

109   Camp Nine's location "within a day's march of the divide" is cited in Joseph P. O'Neil, "Official Report to the Adjutant General on his Exploration of the Olympic Mountains," U.S. Senate, Document No. 59, 54th Congress, p. 8.

109   The statement that O'Neil's men "slept their last night under blankets for almost a moon" is from Fisher, "Lt. O'Neil's Exploration," p. 213.

111   The report that O'Neil gave his speech, standing "beneath the twinkling stars . . . " is from Fisher, "Lt. O'Neil's Exploration," p. 336.

113   The statement that O'Neil divided the expedition's "Southern

Division" is from Fisher, "Lt. O'Neil's Exploration.

Chapter 7

119–120   The quotations in the description of Homan, Hopper, and Maring's trip are from C. C. Maring, "In the Olympic Mountains," *Recreation Magazine* 8, 2 (February 1898), p. 92.

120   Gannett's comment to Dodwell and Rixon, "There's your work, boys . . . " is from Lois Crisler, *The Pacific Coast Ranges: The Wilderness Mountains,* ed. R. Peattie (New York: The Vanguard Press, 1946), p. 201.

122   The statements that the reserve had timber "sufficient to supply the entire United States . . . " and that the peninsula was "the most heavily forested region of Washington . . . " are from Arthur Dodwell and Theodore F. Rixon, *Forest Conditions in the Olympic Forest Reserve, Washington,* United States Geological Survey, Department of the

Interior (Washington, D.C.: GPO, 1902), p. 14.

124 The comment that McGlone often climbed a peak "just to have a look around" is from Crisler, *Pacific Coast Ranges,* p. 202.

124 The name "Elwha Pass" appeared in "The Olympics," *Seattle Press,* July 16, 1890, p. 1, col. 3.

125–126 The quotations in the description of Humes's attempt on Mount Olympus are from G. W. Humes, "Journey to Mount Olympus," *The Mountaineer* 1, 2 (June 1907), pp. 41–42.

127 The Mountaineers' decision to schedule an annual "summer outing" is recorded in "The Ascent of Mt. Olympus," *The Mountaineer* 1, 1 (March 1907).

129–130 The quotations in the description of the Explorers Club ascent of Mount Olympus are from "The Scaling of Olympus," *Port Angeles Tribune-Times,* August 2, 1907.

Chapter 8

131 The identification of the Mountaineers' members as representing "almost every trade and profession" is from *The Mountaineer* 1, 2 (June 1907), p. 53.

132 The description of the trail into the Elwha Basin as "one of the most beautiful in the state" is from "The Mountaineers' Annual Outing, 1907: Announcement of Final Plans for the Olympic Expedition, 1907," *The Mountaineer* 1, 2 (June 1907), p. 46.

133–134 The descriptions of suitable clothing are from "The Ascent of Mt. Olympus," *The Mountaineer* 1, 1 (March 1907), pp. 23–24, and "The Mountaineers' Annual Outing, 1907 . . . ," *The Mountaineer* 1, 2 (June 1907), p. 47.

135 The statement that Humes knew "where the way had been cleared" is from Mary Banks, "Mountaineers in the Olympics," *The Mountaineer* 1, 3 (September 1907), p. 75.

136–139 Unless otherwise noted below, the quotations in the description of the Mountaineers' outing (up to their arrival at the temporary campsite in Queets Basin) are from Banks, "Mountaineers in the Olympics."

139 The addition of the statement "We salute the brave pioneers . . . " to the record left in the cairn is from "Mount Olympus," *The Mountaineer* 1, 3 (September 1907), p. 83.

139 The quotations in the description of The Mountaineers' first attempt on Mount Olympus are from Asahel Curtis, "Storm Bound on Mount Olympus," *The Mountaineer* 1, 3 (September 1907), pp. 69–72.

142 The identification of those who had started out on July 24 as "first comers" is from Banks, "Mountaineers in the Olympics."

142–144 The inscriptions on the magazine page are cited in "Record Found on the Pass Between the Elwha and the Queets," *The Mountaineer* 1, 3 (September 1907), p. 86.

143–147   The quotations in the description of the August 13 ascent are from L. A. Nelson, "The Ascent of Mount Olympus," *The Mountaineer* 1, 3 (September 1907), pp. 65–67.

147   The listing of what was left in the record box is from "Record of Ascents to the Summits of Peaks of the Olympic Range, Made by Members of the Mountaineers in 1907," *The Mountaineer* 1, 3 (September 1907), p. 83.

149   Unless otherwise noted below, the quotations in the description of the 1913 outing are from Gertrude Streator, "The Olympic Outing—1913," *The Mountaineer* 6 (1913), pp. 22, 25, 30.

149   The statement that both ascent and descent were "without incident . . . " and that "more than one conqueror of Olympus appeared half drowned . . . " are from Marion Randall Parsons, "The Ascent of Mount Olympus," *The Mountaineer* 6 (1913), p. 41.

149   The agreement between Wright and Fromme "that another Olympic outing should not be conducted until the so-called Promise Creek trail was in readiness . . . " is reported in Winona Bailey, "Third Olympic Outing," *The Mountaineer* 13, 1 (November 1920), p. 9.

150   The quotations in the description of the 1920 outing are from Bailey, "Third Olympic Outing," pp. 13, 16.

151–153   The quotations in the description of the 1926 outing are from Edmond S. Meany Jr., "1926 Summer Outing in the Olympics," *The Mountaineer* 19, 1 (December 1926), pp. 7, 10, 11, 14.

Epilogue

154   The phrase "notable mountains and landmarks" is from "The 'Press' Explorations," *Seattle Press,* July 16, 1890, p. 20, col. 2.

156   Humphrey reported on his attempt to establish a "national game preserve . . . not only to preserve the game, but as a step toward a national park" in the Hon. W. E. Humphrey, "Olympic National Monument," *The Mountaineer* 2 (November 1909), p. 41.

Selected Bibliography

Books

Bancroft, Hubert Howe. *History of the Northwest Coast—Volume I, 1543–1800*. Volume 27 of *The Works of Hubert Howe Bancroft*. San Francisco: A. L. Bancroft & Company, 1884.

———. *History of the Northwest Coast—Volume II, 1800–1846*. Volume 27 of *The Works of Hubert Howe Bancroft*. San Francisco: The History Company, 1886.

———. *History of Oregon—Volume I, 1834-1848*. Volume 24 of *The Works of Hubert Howe Bancroft*. San Francisco: The History Company, Publishers, 1886.

Cleland, Lucile H. *Trails and Trials of the Pioneers of the Olympic Peninsula*. The Humptulips Pioneer Association, 1959. Facsimile Reproduction, Seattle: The Shorey Book Store, 1973.

Dodwell, Arthur, and Rixon, Theodore F. *Forest Conditions in the Olympic Forest Reserve, Washington*. United States Geological Survey, Department of the Interior. Washington, D.C.: GPO, 1902.

Lauridsen, G. M., and Smith, A. A. *The Story of Port Angeles*. Seattle: Lowman & Hanford Co., 1937.

Meany, Edmond S. *Origin of Washington Geographic Names*. Seattle: University of Washington Press, 1923.

Putnam, George Palmer. *In the Oregon Country*. New York and London: G. P. Putnam's Sons, 1915.

Speck, Gordon. *Northwest Explorations*. Portland: Binford & Mort, 1954.

Wood, Robert L. *Across the Olympic Mountains: The Press Expedition, 1889-90*. Seattle: The Mountaineers and the University of Washington Press, 1967.

———. *Men, Mules, and Mountains: Lieutenant O'Neil's Olympic Expeditions*. Seattle: The Mountaineers, 1976.

———. *Trail Country: Olympic National Park*. Seattle: The Mountaineers, 1968.

Pamphlets and Articles

Albertson, Charles, "Into the Olympics: Our Seventh Annual Outing." *The Mountaineer* 5 (1912).

Alcorn, Gordon D., and Alcorn, Rowena L. "Evergreen on the Queets." *Oregon Historical Quarterly* 74,1 (March 1973).

Bailey, Winona. "The Third Olympic Outing." *The Mountaineer* 13, 1 (November 1920).

Banks, Mary. "Mountaineers in the Olympics." *The Mountaineer* 1, 3 (September 1907).

Bretherton, Bernard J. "Ascent of Mount Olympus." *Steel Points* (Portland) 1, 4 (July 1907).

———. "Elk and Camera." *Overland*

Monthly 35, 206 (February 1900).

Browne, Belmore. "The First Ascent of Mount Olympus." *Bulletin of the American Geographical Society* 42, 12 (1910).

Christie, J. H. "From the Leader of the Press Expedition." *The Mountaineer* 19, 1 (December 1926).

"Copy of Record Found in Elwha Pass." *The Mountaineer* 1, 3 (September 1907).

Curtis, Asahel. "Storm Bound on Mount Olympus." *The Mountaineer* 1, 3 (September 1907).

———. "The First Ascent of Mount Olympus." *The World's Work* (May 1908).

"First Annual Outing, Members of Party." *The Mountaineer* 1, 3 (September 1907).

Flett, J. B. "Observations on the Olympics." *The Mountaineer* 1, 2 (June 1907).

Fromme, Rudo L. "The Olympic National Forest—What It Means." *The Mountaineer* 6 (1913).

Gauld, Charles A. "Mt. Anderson and General Anderson." Washington, D.C.: Charles A. Gauld, 1941.

———. "Thomas M. Anderson: First U.S. General Overseas." *Clark County History* (Fort Vancouver Historical Society) 14 (1973).

Gilman, S. C. "The Olympic Region." *West Shore,* July 7, 1890.

Gilman, S. C., and Gilman, C. A. "The Olympic Country." *National Geographic,* April 4, 1896.

Hanna, Ina M. "Expeditions into the Olympic Mountains." *The Mountaineer* 1, 2 (June 1907).

Henderson, Louis F. "Flora of the Olympics." *Steel Points* (Portland) 1, 4 (July 1907). Reprinted from ZOE 2, No. 3 (October 1891).

Himes, George H. "First Ascent of Mount Olympus." *Steel Points* (Portland) 1, 4 (July 1907).

Hitchman, Robert B. "Name Calling." *The Mountaineer* 52, 4 (March 1959).

Humes, G. W. "Journey to Mount Olympus." *The Mountaineer* 1, 2 (June 1907).

Landes, Henry. "Notes on the Geography of the Olympics." *The Mountaineer* 1, 2 (June 1907).

Lange, Erwin F. "Pioneer Botanists of the Pacific Northwest." *Oregon Historical Quarterly* 57, 2 (June 1956).

Maring, C. C. "In the Olympic Mountains." *Recreation Magazine* 8, 2 (February 1898).

Meany, Edmond S. "The Olympic National Monument." *The Mountaineer* 4 (1911).

———. "The Olympics in History and Legend." *The Mountaineer* 6 (1913).

———. "Indians of the Olympic Peninsula." *The Mountaineer* 13, 1 (November 1920).

———. "The Story of Three Olympic Peaks." *Washington Historical*

Quarterly 4, 3 (1913).

Meany, Edmond S., Jr. "1926 Summer Outing in the Olympics." *The Mountaineer* 19, 1 (December 1926).

"Members of the 1920 Outing." *The Mountaineer* 13, 1 (November 1920).

"Members of the 1926 Summer Outing." *The Mountaineer* 19, 1 (December 1926).

"Mountaineers in the Olympics." *The Mountaineer* 1, 3 (September 1907).

Nelson, L. A. "Mount Meany." *The Mountaineer* 13, 1 (November 1920).

———. "The Ascent of Mount Olympus." *The Mountaineer* 1, 3 (September 1907).

"Names in the Olympic Region." *Steel Points* 1, 4 (July 1907).

Parsons, Marion Randall. "The Ascent of Mount Olympus." *The Mountaineer* 6 (1913).

Putnam, W. T. "Lake Cushman as a Summer Resort." *Washington* 1, 3 (May 1906).

"Record of Ascents." *The Mountaineer* 1, 3 (September 1907).

"Record of Mountains Climbed on Olympus Outing, 1913." *The Mountaineer* 6 (1913).

Smith, A. A. "The Olympics." *Steel Points* (Portland) 1, 4 (July 1907).

Streator, Gertrude. "The Olympic Outing—1913." *The Mountaineer* 6 (1913).

———. "Triple Peaked Olympus Has Three Records." *The Mountaineer* 13, 1 (November 1920).

"The Ascent of Mt. Olympus." *The Mountaineer* 1, 1 (March 1907).

"The Mountaineers' Annual Outing, 1907: Announcement of the Final Plans for the Olympic Expedition." *The Mountaineer* 1, 2 (June 1907).

Weaver, Charles E. "Notes on the Bed Rock Geology of the Olympic Peninsula." *The Mountaineer* 1, 3 (September 1907).

Weer, Harry. "Ascent of Mount Meany, August 13, 1913." *The Mountaineer* 6 (1913).

Wickersham, James. "A National Park in the Olympics . . . 1890." *The Living Wilderness* 77 (Summer-Fall 1961).

Newspaper Articles

Hoquiam Washingtonian:

October 9, 1890. "O'Neil's Olympian Empire Edition."

Mason County Journal:

May 2, 1890. "Exploring the Quinault."

June 13, 1890. S. C. Gilman, "The Olympic Peninsula."

August 15, 1890. Frederic Church, "The Lake Cushman Copper Mines."

Port Angeles Tribune-Times:

August 2, 1907. "The Scaling of Olympus."

Portland Oregonian:

June 16, 1887. Elwood Evans, "Michael T. Simmons."

August 4, 1888. "The Oregon Alpine Club."

July 8, 1889. "The City of Port Angeles."

October 26, 1889. "A Chance for an Explorer." (Reprinted from the *Seattle Press*)

March 11, 1890. "Strange Indian Tribe."

April 15, 1890. "The Olympic Range."

May 11, 1890. "The Quillayute Country."

May 25, 1890. "The Olympic Peninsula."

June 3, 1890. "The Olympic Range."

June 25, 1890. "Ho for the Olympics."

July 2, 1890. "The Olympic Gateway."

July 2, 1890. "The Alpine Club's Expedition."

July 19, 1890. F. J. Church, "Olympic Explorers."

September 7, 1890. "Thro' the Olympics."

October 10, 1890. "The O'Neil Banquet."

October 20, 1890. "The O'Neil Banquet."

October 23, 1890. "A Brilliant Banquet."

November 4, 1890. "The Expedition Came High."

December 1, 1890. "At the Playhouse. Lieutenant O'Neil's Lecture."

December 6, 1890. "Lieutenant O'Neil's Lecture Tonight."

Seattle Press:

July 16, 1890. "The Olympics." "The Press Trail." "The Nomenclature." "Geology of the Olympics." "Christie's Journal." "O'Neil's Exploration—Record of his trip back of Port Angeles in 1885." "Semple's Striking Report." "Belittling Lieut. O'Neil." "They Found the Trail." "The City of Port Angeles." "To the Northwest Press."

Seattle Post-Intelligencer:

June 5, 1890. S. C. Gilman, "Unknown No Longer."

June 6, 1890. "The Gilman Discovery."

June 25, 1890. "Off for the Olympics." "The Olympic Vales."

July 1, 1890. "That Unknown Land."

July 14, 1890. B. J. Bretherton, "Gates of the Range."

August 6, 1890. B. J. Bretherton, "The Range Crossed."

August 14, 1890. B. J. Bretherton, "Across the Divide."

September 3, 1890. B. J. Bretherton, "On the Duckabush."

September 19, 1890. B. J. Bretherton, "Exploring the Olympics."

September 28, 1890. "O'Neil's Caravan Emerges."

January 1, 1891. S. C. Gilman, "The Wild Olympic Range."

Shelton-Mason County Journal:

April 13 and 20, May 25, June 15, July 6, August 3 and 17, September 7, October 12 and 19, and December 28, 1950.

February 1, 1951. William T. Putnam, "Stories and People of Old Lake Cushman—Memoirs of a Pioneer."

St. Cloud Journal-Press (Minnesota):

January 16, 1896, "S. C. Gilman Dead."

St. Cloud Daily Times (Minnesota):
June 8, 1927, "Chas. A. Gilman, Aged Pioneer, Dies."

Tacoma Ledger:
July 20, 1890. Frederic Church, "Above Lake Cushman."
August 10, 1890. B. J. Bretherton, "Olympic Explorers."
August 17, 1890. B. J. Bretherton, "Olympic Adventure."
August 24, 1890. B. J. Bretherton, "Olympic Exploration."
September 7, 1890. B. J. Bretherton, "Olympic Exploration."

Diaries, Documents, Manuscripts, and Notes
Banta, John J. "Memorandum of our exploring trip from Tacoma around the Straits of Juan de Fuca to Pysht Bay, and through the country south to Grays Harbor (S. P. Sharp, J. J. Banta), Dec. 3rd, 1889 to Jan. 7th 1890." Collection of Lelia Barney.

Bretherton, Bernard J. Diary kept during 1890 O'Neil expedition. Bretherton Collection, National Park Service, Port Angeles, Washington.
Church, Frederic J. Diary kept during 1890 O'Neil expedition. Robert B. Hitchman Collection, Washington State Historical Society, Tacoma.
Fisher, H. [James B. Hanmore]. "Lt. O'Neil's Exploration of the Olympic Mountains," 1890. Mazamas' library, Portland, Oregon. Transcribed by Robert L. Wood; copy of typescript in University of Washington Libraries Archives.
Fromme, Rudo L. "Fromme's Olympic Memoirs." National Park Service, Port Angeles, Washington.
Henderson, Louis F. "Early Experiences of a Botanist in the Northwest." Manuscript of a talk given before the Oregon Audubon Society in 1932. Special Collections, University of Oregon, Eugene.

Linsley, Nelson E. Report to Lieutenant O'Neil, dated October 3, 1890, regarding exploring trip to Mount Olympus. Robert B. Hitchman Collection, Washington State Historical Society, Tacoma.
Morse, Eldridge. "Notes on the History and Resources of Washington Territory, furnished Hubert Howe Bancroft of San Francisco, California, Volume 19." Bancroft Library, University of California, Berkeley. Photocopy, Hubert Howe Bancroft Collection, University of Washington Libraries.
O'Neil, Joseph P. Handwritten manuscript (with revisions) detailing his explorations. Robert B. Hitchman Collection, Washington State Historical Society, Tacoma.
O'Neil, Joseph P. "Official Report to the Adjutant General on his Exploration of the Olympic Mountains" and "Remarks on the

Olympic Mountains." U. S. Senate, Document No. 59, 54th Congress. National Archives, Washington, D.C.

O'Neil, Joseph P. Unpublished lecture notes (six sets). Robert B. Hitchman Collection, Washington State Historical Society, Tacoma.

Wickersham, James. "Sketches, A Trip to the Olympic Mountains." Handwritten notebook transcribed by George Marshall, University of Alaska at Fairbanks. Photocopy, "George Marshall, Collector" accession, University of Washington Libraries.

Maps

"The Olympic Country, Washington, U.S.A." Topographic map, based in part upon the Gilman explorations, published in *National Geographic*, April 1896.

"Map of the Olympic Mountains explored by the Expedition sent out by 'The Seattle Press' 1890." Charles A. Barnes, topographer. *Seattle Press,* July 16, 1890.

"W. G. Steel's Map of the Olympic Mountains, in Washington, U.S.A., compiled by H. Fisher." Copyright 1891 by W. G. Steel.

Index

About the author

Robert L. Wood first saw the Olympics in 1946 and since then has spent literally thousands of days exploring these intriguing mountains and researching their history. He is the author of five books, including the award-winning *Across the Olympic Mountains*, as well as *Trail Country: Olympic National Park; Wilderness Trails of Olympic National Park; Men, Mules, and Mountains;* and *Olympic Mountains Trail Guide,* now in its second edition. A member of The Mountaineers, the National Parks Association, the Nature Conservancy, the Sierra Club, and the Wilderness Society, he lives in Seattle.

THE MOUNTAINEERS, founded in 1906, is a nonprofit outdoor activity and conservation club, whose mission is "to explore, study, preserve, and enjoy the natural beauty of the outdoors. . . . " Based in Seattle, Washington, the club is now the third-largest such organization in the United States, with 15,000 members and four branches throughout Washington State.

The Mountaineers sponsors both classes and year-round outdoor activities in the Pacific Northwest, which include hiking, mountain climbing, ski-touring, snowshoeing, bicycling, camping, kayaking and canoeing, nature study, sailing, and adventure travel. The club's conservation division supports environmental causes through educational activities, sponsoring legislation, and presenting informational programs. All club activities are led by skilled, experienced volunteers, who are dedicated to promoting safe and responsible enjoyment and preservation of the outdoors.

The Mountaineers Books, an active, nonprofit publishing program of the club, produces guidebooks, instructional texts, historical works, natural history guides, and works on environmental conservation. All books produced by The Mountaineers are aimed at fulfilling the club's mission.

If you would like to participate in these organized outdoor activities or the club's programs, consider a membership in The Mountaineers. For information and an application, write or call The Mountaineers, Club Headquarters, 300 Third Avenue West, Seattle, Washington 98119; (206) 284-6310.

Send or call for our catalog of more than 300 outdoor titles:

The Mountaineers Books
1001 SW Klickitat Way, Suite 201
Seattle, WA 98134
1(800)553-4453